MIDWAY

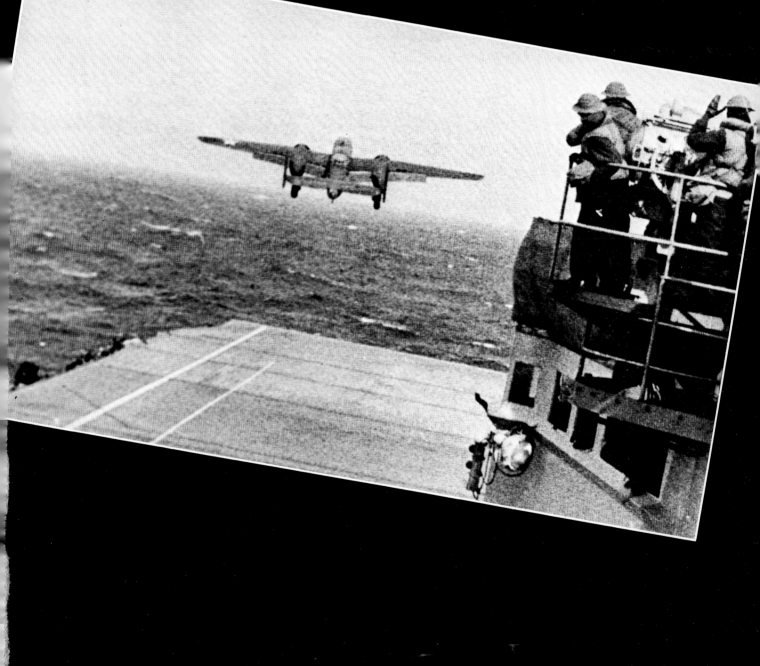

MIDWAY

LT. COL. A. J. BARKER

GALAHAD BOOKS

A Bison Book

First published in the US by
Galahad Books
a division of A&W Publishers, Inc.
95 Madison Avenue
New York
New York 10016

Copyright © 1981 Bison Books Limited

Produced by
Bison Books Limited
4 Cromwell Place
London SW7

Library of Congress Catalog Card Number:
81-80456

ISBN 0-88365-545-4

Printed in Hong Kong

CONTENTS

1. Prologue   6
2. Plans and Preparations   14
3. First Strikes   24
4. Disaster for Nagumo   30
5. The end of the *Yorktown* and *Hiryu*   37
6. Yamamoto's Reaction   46
7. Retreat   51
    Appendix   60
    Index   63

Page 1: A B-25 takes off from the *Hornet* for the Doolittle raid.
Page 2–3: The USS *Enterprise* was one of the major participants in the Battle of Midway.
Page 4–5: The USS *Atlanta* at sea in November 1942. The *Atlanta* Class cruisers had 10 5-inch guns.

1. PROLOGUE

Above: Admiral Chester Nimitz was C in C of the US Pacific Fleet during the Battle of Midway.

Japan's daring attack on Pearl Harbor on 7 December 1941 was a catastrophic surprise for the United States which compelled a radical change in both American and Japanese strategy. Admiral Kimmel was replaced as Commander in Chief of the Pacific Fleet by a keen-witted, blue-eyed Texan, Admiral Chester W Nimitz, and his primary task was defined as the holding of a line running between Hawaii and the vital American base at Midway Island, 1100 miles southwest of Pearl Harbor. He also was instructed to maintain communications with and between America and Australia. The United States was determined, at this point, to prevent a further Japanese advance toward the west, but not to attack.

Since Pearl Harbor the Japanese High Command had been so engrossed in the problem of acquiring oil that, with the exception of Admiral Isoruku Yamamoto, Commander in Chief of Japan's Combined Fleet, it had given little thought to a long-term strategic plan. However by March 1942 a brilliant run of success had given Japan all the oil she needed. The war, it seemed, was going well. Japan's initial objectives had been gained without a hitch and all that remained was to determine her

future strategy. Should she concentrate on stabilizing what she had won, or should she allow the tide of victory to sweep her forward into new territories? And if so, where? Should she strike westward toward India and join hands with her Axis ally somewhere in the Middle East? Or should she concentrate her strength on a drive eastward against the United States? It was difficult to determine which course would be more effective and, if there was to be an offensive, which would be the most productive in terms of economic gain.

Following considerable and often heated deliberations the Japanese Supreme Command concluded that whatever strategy was adopted it would have to be implemented quickly. The Americans were known to be anxious to avenge Pearl Harbor and without some definite plan of action Japan might well be caught. Theoretically the planning of naval strategy was the responsibility of the Chief of the Naval Staff, Admiral Osami Nagano, who was senior to Yamamoto but Nagano's authority had declined after Pearl Harbor and by January 1942 the influence of Yamamoto and his staff was paramount and unquestioned. Thus it is not surprising that Yamamoto's headquarters should take the initiative and that the plan of action which emerged bore the stamp of the man responsible for the attack on Pearl Harbor.

At a series of conferences aboard Yamamoto's flagship, the giant battleship *Yamato,* various alternatives were considered. Seizure of the US Pacific Fleet base and of the Pacific Fleet itself would constitute the most damaging blow to the United States, claimed Rear Admiral Matome Ugaki, Yamamoto's zealous Chief of Staff. So an offensive should be directed against Hawaii. Such an operation, he maintained, would probably provoke a decisive clash with the US Pacific Fleet, in which Japan's superiority in aircraft carriers and battleships should weigh the outcome in her favor. Those who argued against this plan maintained it would be impossible to get a Japanese fleet within striking distance of Hawaii because it would have to pass within striking distance of the island of Midway, and Midway acted as a long-distance outpost to Hawaii. The garrison there would be sure to alert the US Pacific Fleet, so eliminating any hope of achieving surprise as at Pearl Harbor.

Another alternative that was considered was a 'go-west' plan, whose success depended on the destruction of the British Far Eastern Fleet and the capture of Ceylon. The Japanese army commanders opposed this on the grounds that an attack on Ceylon would necessitate moving troops from Burma and Malaya. The third alternative, proposed by Captain Sadatoshi Tomioka, head of the Naval General Staff's Plans Division, was that Australia should be Japan's next major objective. This was rejected by the army even more quickly than the proposed invasion of Ceylon. The Army High Command said such an operation against Australia would require a minimum force of 10 combat divisions and they could not be spared.

At this point Yamamoto decided to show his hand. Up to now he had refrained from voicing any opinion during the planning conferences. Now, reports of the increasing activity of US aircraft carriers and submarines were causing him considerable concern. Midway was an important forward fuelling point for US submarines. Its capture would limit their activities and the establishment of a Japanese air base there should also do much to curb the activities of American carrier-borne aircraft. A move against Midway was the first phase of Ugaki's plan for the invasion of Hawaii but it was not this which interested Yamamoto. He knew that he must lure out and annihilate the US Pacific Fleet in 1942 or Japan would lose the war. Midway, he reasoned, provided ideal bait. Admiral Nimitz could not let Hawaii's sentry fall by default and whatever he chose to do about it would involve a move of the US Pacific Fleet westward to a point where the Combined Fleet could strike. Yamamoto was, in fact, merely pursuing his old dream. By destroying the American aircraft carriers, capturing Midway and threatening Hawaii he believed that America's will to fight would be undermined and the way for a negotiated peace would be opened up.

Thus it was that at the beginning of April Yamamoto's operations staff officer, Commander Yasuji Watanabe was sent to Tokyo to present the plan of Operation MI against Midway to the Naval General Staff. The admirals in Tokyo were bitterly opposed to it, but Yamamoto – the most important admiral in the Imperial Navy – was determined not to be put off, and the Naval

Below right: Vice-Admiral Chuichi Nagumo led the carriers of the Main Striking Force at Midway.
Below far right: Rear Admiral Aubrey Fitch commanded the Task Force 11 at the Battle of the Coral Sea.
Bottom: The Japanese battleship *Yamato* was the largest ship of its kind and was Yamamoto's flagship at Midway.
Below: Admiral Isoroku Yamamoto devised the Japanese assault on Midway Island.

General Staff reluctantly sanctioned the operation.

Meanwhile, as the detailed plan of Operation MI was being worked out, Vice-Admiral Nagumo, commanding the First Air Fleet, was engaged in operations around Ceylon which resulted in the sinking of two British heavy cruisers and the aircraft carrier HMS *Hermes*. In consequence neither he nor Vice-Admiral Kondo whose Second Fleet was similarly engaged in operations around Malaya were consulted regarding the battle plan. This proved to be

a mistake because these two fleets were scheduled to play a leading role in the forthcoming operation. However, most of the wrangling over the plan was about when the operation would take place. Yamamoto favored an attack in the middle of May, while the Naval General Staff wanted it postponed until June in order to allow three more weeks' preparation.

It was now that two dramatic events occurred which affected both the timing and the probable outcome of the forthcoming battle of Midway. Of these the

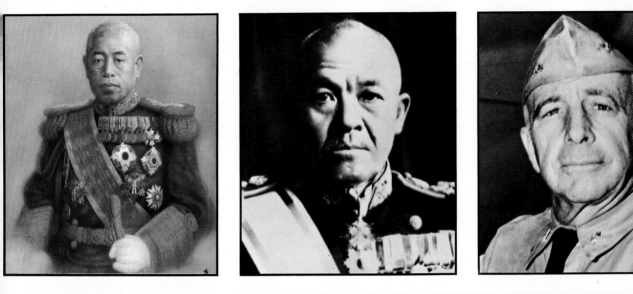

most important was the Americans' first defensive success in what is now known as the Battle of the Coral Sea – the first naval action in history fought almost entirely between aircraft carriers. The battle took place nearly 3000 miles from Midway on the northern approaches to Australia. Following Nagumo's sortie against Ceylon the Japanese had dispatched an invasion force to sail around the eastern end of New Guinea to take Port Moresby on the southern coast. Success of this venture would have meant that the Japanese would have secured the western approach to the Coral Sea. However, cryptographers in the US Navy had broken Japan's most secret code and the Americans had prior notice of the Coral Sea invasion, and guessed correctly that the main strike would be aimed at Port Moresby.

Above far left: A prewar shot of the carrier USS *Lexington* (CV-2), sunk during the Battle of the Coral Sea.
Above left: The Japanese *Shokaku* was damaged by US Navy dive bombers at Coral Sea, but managed to return to Japan for repairs.
Below: Shoho was not so fortunate, her sinking being marked by the famous signal 'Scratch one flattop.'

Left: Doolittle (fourth from left) led the audacious Tokyo raid by B-25 bombers flying from *Hornet.*
Below left: the Douglas SBD Dauntless dive bomber (foreground) and the TBD Devastator torpedo bomber provided American carriers with striking power at the Midway and Coral Sea battles.
Right: USS *Lexington* ablaze after receiving hits from two bombs and two torpedoes on 8 May 1942 in the Coral Sea.
Below: Lexington is abandoned by her crew as the fires aboard become uncontrollable. She was later sent to the bottom by torpedoes from US destroyers.

The Doolittle raid on the Japanese
homeland on 18 April 1942 was
important as a boost to American
morale, rather than for its material
effects. USAAF North American B-25
Mitchell bombers were launched from
the carrier USS *Hornet* (CV-8) in one
of the most remarkable feats of
airmanship of World War II.

On 3 May the Japanese staged successful landings on Tulagi, but were bombed and strafed the next day by planes from the carrier USS *Yorktown*. The *Yorktown* then rendezvoused with the carrier *Lexington*, and a course was fixed for a surprise attack on the Japanese invasion forces now rounding the end of New Guinea. On 7 May a destroyer and an oiler, separated from the main US forces, were destroyed by Japanese carrier planes. The same day aircraft from *Lexington* and *Yorktown* caught the Japanese light carrier *Shoho*, and sank her. The next day, 8 May, aircraft from the two big Japanese carriers, *Shokaku* and *Zuikaku*, traded air attacks with the two US carriers. *Shokaku* was severely damaged and *Zuikaku* lost a number of first-class fighting planes and pilots. The *Lexington* sustained several bomb and torpedo hits. The damage seemed to have been brought under control, and it was not until some time later that fires and explosions broke out; a motor generator had been left running, igniting gasoline vapors released by an earlier torpedo hit. The condition of the ship worsened until, in the evening, the *Lexington* had to be abandoned. She was then torpedoed by one of her own escorting destroyers.

No clear-cut victory could be claimed by either side. However the Americans had forced the Japanese to turn back their invasion forces from Port Moresby, and two of the big Japanese carriers were damaged so badly they would not be on hand for the forthcoming battle of Midway – where they just might have turned the tide.

The other event which had a profound effect on the battle occurred before the Coral Sea action could take place. Indeed, although Midway was fought between 3 June and 6 June 1942, it was precipitated six weeks before, on 18 April. At 0800 that morning Vice-Admiral William F Halsey sent a signal from his flagship, the carrier *Enterprise*, then 650 miles off Tokyo, to Captain Marc Mitscher of the carrier *Hornet* nearby. The signal read, 'Launch planes. To Colonel Doolittle and his gallant command Good Luck and God bless you.'

As the Americans had hoped, Doolittle's raid on Tokyo deceived the Japanese into assuming that Doolittle's B-25 bombers – which had never flown from a carrier before – had taken off from a land base. President Roosevelt himself announced jocosely that the raiders had flown from 'Shangri-La.' Officers of the Imperial General Staff measured their charts. Except for the sterile and unlikely Aleutians, the American outpost nearest Tokyo was Midway Island, 2250 miles eastward. Not only must this be Shangri-La, the Japanese concluded, but it was additionally dangerous as 'a sentry for Hawaii,' 1140 miles farther. So it must be eliminated. Thus Yamamoto got his way and by the middle of May the ships chosen for Operation MI – Midway Island – were being mustered from the fringes of the empire.

2. PLANS AND PREPARATIONS

At the beginning of May the first draft of the plan for Operation MI was formally submitted to Admiral Nagano, Chief of the Imperial Naval Staff. It was approved and on 5 May an Imperial directive was issued ordering the Commander in Chief of the Combined Fleet to, 'carry out the occupation of Midway Island and key points in the western Aleutians, in cooperation with the Army.' The army was to provide an infantry regimental group for the assault landing on Midway. No specific date was set for the operation but the directive noted that operations would begin during 'the first 20 days of June.'

Thus it was that toward the end of the first week in May the largest fleet in the history of naval warfare began to assemble in Japanese waters. Its backbone was to be the Carrier Striking Force of four big carriers, *Akagi*, *Kaga*, *Hiryu* and *Soryu*. These were to be under command of Vice-Admiral Chuichi Nagumo, flying his flag in the *Akagi* and screened by the two fast battleships *Kirishima* and *Haruna*, two heavy and one light cruisers, and 11 destroyers. This was the force which was to track down and destroy the US Pacific Fleet. The remainder of the Combined Fleet was divided into four groups: the Submarine Advance Expeditionary Force which would take up positions before the other groups went into action; a Midway Occupation Force; a Northern Area Force; and the so-called 'Main Body' under the

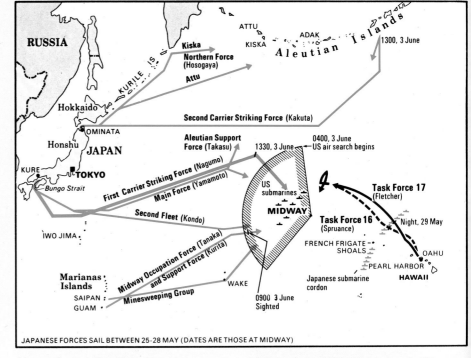

JAPANESE FORCES SAIL BETWEEN 25-28 MAY (DATES ARE THOSE AT MIDWAY)

Above: A map showing Japan's moves against Midway and American dispositions for the defense of the island in May/June 1942.
Below right: The *Kongo* was with the Midway Occupation Force.
Below: Kaga sailed with the Japanese First Carrier Striking Force.

Above right: USAAF Boeing B-17 Flying Fortresses operated from Midway Island during the battle, a prewar formation being shown.
Right: Martin B-26 Marauder medium bombers were also based on Midway.

personal command of Admiral Yamamoto.

The submarines were an essential part of the plan. One of them was to reconnoiter ahead for the Midway Occupation Force, while four stationed themselves off the Aleutians and two others off America's west coast. Others were to cover Pearl Harbor – four taking up positions 500 miles west of Oahu and another seven across the route between Pearl and Midway. All were to be in position by 1 June. With these submarines in wait, west and north of Hawaii, Yamamoto presumed that in the absence of other sources of information he would have ample warning when ships of the Pacific Fleet were moving out to meet him. After radioing their reports the submarines could then attack and, hopefully, inflict the first losses in the 'one decisive action.'

Admiral Nobutake Kondo, who had played a leading part in the invasion of the Dutch East Indies, was nominated as commander of the Midway Occupation Force and he was to be responsible for the capture of the island. Under his command were two battleships, the light carrier *Zuiho*, eight cruisers and nine destroyers to escort the invasion force of 15 troopships carrying some 5000 soldiers. Vice-Admiral Moshiro Hosogaya was given command of the Northern Area Force, whose striking element rested on two carriers, the *Ryujo* and the new *Junyo*, under command of Rear-Admiral Kaukuji Kakuda. It was hoped that the Aleutian landings would divert American attention from Midway, and Hosogaya's Main Force was to station itself halfway between Midway and the Aleutians to intercept any American force coming from either direction.

The Main Body centered on seven giant battleships, including Yamamoto's flagship *Yamato*, from which he would direct the battle. The *Yamato* and her sister ship, the *Musashi*, both mounted 18 11-inch guns and were the most formidable warships in the world. Air cover for his force was provided by the old light carrier *Hosho*.

Altogether Yamamoto had 700 aircraft

nd 200 ships – among them 11 battleships, ight carriers, 22 cruisers, 65 destroyers and o submarines. The total displacement of hese ships exceeded 1,500,000 tons and hey were manned by 100,000 officers and nen, many of whom were veterans of ctions in the Pacific and Indian Oceans. Yamamoto's main force of battleships was o be 600 miles northwest of Midway and creened by a large detachment under Vice-Admiral Takasu 500 miles north of Midway. Nagumo's carriers were to be tationed approximately 300 miles east of Yamamoto.

In terms of relative strength at the end of April Yamamoto had almost three times as many carriers as the Americans had. Against he four carriers currently believed to be available to Admiral Nimitz – *Yorktown*, *Saratoga*, *Hornet* and *Enterprise* – the Combined Fleet boasted seven large and our light carriers. The USS *Saratoga*, thought by the Japanese to be a threat, was in fact undergoing repairs in Puget Sound at the time of the battle. In view of this comfortable margin of superiority Yamamoto's main worry was that the Americans would refuse battle with such an invincible armada. Unlike the Americans he was limited by lack of information, for his intelligence officers had no clue as to where the American carriers might be.

Yamamoto's overall plan was for the Northern Area Force to open the battle. Twenty-four hours before the Midway invasion Kakuta's two carriers, the *Ryujo* and *Junyo*, would deliver a paralyzing air bombardment on Dutch Harbor, and troops would then land on Adak, Attu and Kiska. This operation was intended to confuse Admiral Nimitz as to the Japanese intentions. The invasion was not intended to be a permanent affair, and Yamamoto wanted to withdraw his troops in mid-September, before winter set in.

At dawn the following day, Nagumo's big carriers would bomb Midway and, hopefully, destroy the American aircraft there. If the Pacific Fleet tried to interfere Nagumo would deliver the first blow against it. Meanwhile Yamamoto's main force would be moving to a position to the west for the finale. Simultaneously, after dusk on D-Day +1, the Midway Occupation Force would be put ashore by Admiral Kondo, and the first objective of the operation would have been attained.

By the end of April many of the ships that were to take part in the Midway operation had assembled in the Inland Sea; the focal

point of all activity was the Hashirajima Anchorage in Hiroshima Bay. With the exception of the two giant carriers, *Zuikaku* and *Shokaku*, and their escorting vessels, Admiral Nagumo's Fleet had returned from its triumphant sweep round Ceylon two days after Doolittle's raid. It was not until 1 May that Nagumo, the Carrier Group commander, and Vice-Admiral Kondo, who was to escort the troopships, reported to Yamamoto aboard his bustling flagship. Only then did Nagumo, Kondo and the senior officers who had accompanied them for the briefing, learn about the proposed operation. Reactions were mixed. Nagumo was openly indifferent to the plan and the location of the operation. However Kondo had serious misgivings. He believed that the operation was doomed to failure because the Americans would employ substantial numbers of land-based aircraft against the Japanese forces as well as their whole carrier fleet. Yamamoto was in no mood to listen to Kondo and curtly dismissed his views.

Throughout May preparations were rushed forward for the coming operation. Dummy bombing and torpedo attacks were practiced on the hulk of the old 21,000-ton battleship *Settsu*, anchored at Iwakuni in the Inland Sea. Many of the pilots' practice attacks proved so disappointing that the staff officers supervising the training openly wondered how such poor aviators would ever equal the feats of their forerunners at Pearl Harbor. As they were not given enough time to practice, even their flying formations were ragged. Admiral Ugaki also staged a series of war games to test Yamamoto's command and control structure. The result was that at the end of the games Admiral Kondo, backed by most of the other admirals, urged that the invasion day be postponed to allow more time for the training of pilots and staff officers as well as for the battle preparations. Once again Yamamoto refused to listen. He insisted that early June was the only time when there would be enough moonlight for the night movements off the invasion beaches.

Another important matter that was raised was the problem of inadequate radio equipment aboard the carrier *Akagi*. The need to keep radio masts small and unobtrusive, so that they would not interfere with the landing and takeoff of the carrier's planes, meant that this problem was not peculiar to the *Akagi*. However, the *Akagi* was Nagumo's flagship and as Rear Admiral Kusaka, Nagumo's Chief of Staff, pointed out, it was vital that the *Akagi* should be able to intercept enemy radio messages. Two remedies were suggested. The first was that Yamamoto's flagship the *Yamato*, with its modern and powerful radio installations, should ignore the radio silence imposed on the rest of the fleet and relay all important intercepted messages to the *Akagi*. The second was that the *Yamato* should operate directly with the carriers, with Yamamoto

assuming direct command of the Nagumo Force. Both suggestions were rejected.

This was but one of the important problems that were still left unanswered when the war games broke up. Many officers returned to their ships dissatisfied and uneasy. The only people, it seems, who were not unduly worried were Nagumo and his flying crews. They almost believed themselves capable of smashing the US Pacific Fleet on their own.

Shortly before the Coral Sea battle US Intelligence informed Admiral Nimitz that the Japanese offensive named Operation MI was about to be launched. The objective, according to intercepted signals, was somewhere labelled 'AF.' The intelligence officers who worked in the Intelligence Black Chamber at Pearl Harbor where Japanese secret messages were monitored and decoded, were not sure whether 'AF' was Midway or Oahu and whether D-Day would be at the end of May or in early June. Nimitz felt certain that it would be Midway and on 2 May he flew there from Pearl Harbor.

Midway is devoid of nearly all the attributes usually associated with South Sea Islands. The entire atoll is only six miles in diameter and very little of that is dry land. Of its two islets, Sand and Eastern, the first is less than two miles long and the other is little more than one. In the middle is a lagoon with a narrow ships channel leading into it, and on the western edge is an open harbor of sorts. All in all it is a miserable flyspeck of land, but since the attack on Pearl Harbor in December 1941 it was the most westerly American base in the Pacific.

On 2 May 1942 Admiral Nimitz inspected the installations on Sand and Eastern Islands accompanied by Lieutenant Colonel Harold Shannon, the Commanding officer of the 6th Marine Defense Battalion, and Commander Cyril Simard, who was in charge of the naval air station. Each island was self-contained, with its own barracks, power supply and support facilities. The chief difference between the two was that all the facilities needed for the airplanes, except the seaplane hangars, were located on Eastern Island. It was a hot day, but Nimitz thoroughly inspected the military installations, looking at gun sites, ammunition dumps, barbed wire and underground command posts. He told neither Shannon or Simard of his theories about the impending attack but before leaving he asked Shannon what equipment he needed to withstand 'a large-scale attack.' When Shannon had listed what was required, Nimitz reemphasized his point, 'If I get you all these things you say you need, can you hold Midway against a major amphibious assault?' Shannon assured Nimitz that he could.

Shortly after his return to Oahu, Nimitz wrote a joint letter to Shannon and Simard. He said he had confidence in them and was recommending their promotion. The

Japanese, he continued, were mounting a large-scale offensive against Midway, which was expected to be launched on 28 May. He informed them that he was rushing every man, gun and plane he could spare to Midway. He hoped it would be enough.

Following this letter everything that could be done to strengthen the atoll's defenses was put under way. Shannon's garrison now numbered 2138 Marines and Simand's fliers and ancillary troops totalled 1494. More antiaircraft guns were installed, the beaches had literally been covered with barbed wire and both the shore and sea approaches to it were heavily mined. Every position had been equipped with Molotov cocktails; arrangements had been completed for 11 torpedo boats to circle the reefs and patrol the lagoon; and finally, 19 submarines had been stationed to guard the approaches to the island from the southwest to the north, some at 100 miles, some at 150 miles and the rest at 200 miles.

By 3 June the ground defenses of Midway were as complete as they ever would be. Before the Japanese could establish a beachhead, they would have to smash those defenses. Nonetheless Simard and Shannon were worried. If Yamamoto's battleships and cruisers stood offshore, under an umbrella of Zeros provided by his aircraft carriers, and subjected Midway to an all-out bombardment it would take a lot of planes to beat them off. Nimitz had increased Midway's aircraft strength and by 3 June there 121 on the island. However 30 of them were reconnaissance aircraft, Catalina PBYs, slow, vulnerable and almost useless in combat and 37 of the other fighters and dive bombers were obsolete machines. Moreover most of the new pilots had only just completed their flying training and none of those who flew the dive bombers had had any practice in dive bombing. Worst perhaps was the fact that some of the pilots and crews were from the army, some from the navy and some were Marine. In those days interservice liaison was little more than wishful thinking.

Nimitz had done his best for Midway's land-based garrison. The US Commander in Chief knew full well that the islands' fate depended not on its troops and planes but on the Pacific Fleet which was desperately short of aircraft carriers. *Lexington* had been sunk and *Yorktown* severely damaged in the Coral Sea battle, and it did not look as if she could be repaired in time to help defend Midway. *Saratoga* was still at San Diego undergoing repairs from a torpedo attack by a Japanese submarine in January.

With *Lexington* definitely out of the running and *Yorktown* and *Saratoga* doubtful starters, Nimitz had only the *Hornet* and the *Enterprise*. Both were at sea patrolling the South Pacific between Pearl Harbor and the Coral Sea when they received orders to return to Pearl Harbor. The damaged *Yorktown* was also making for Pearl Harbor and on 27 May – the day after Nagumo's four carriers left the Inland Sea –

Above: Admiral William Halsey, one of the US Navy's leading exponents of carrier warfare, missed the Battle of Midway through ill health.
Below: Admiral Chester Nimitz visited Midway Island on a tour of inspection shortly after the battle ended.
Above right: Douglas TBD Devastators suffered heavy losses at Midway.
Above far right: Consolidated PBY Catalina flying boats performed a vital reconnaissance role.
Right: The carrier USS *Yorktown* survived the Battle of the Coral Sea to provide a much-needed contribution to the defense of Midway Island.

the *Yorktown* crept into dry dock there. (For the Japanese it was 28 May not 27 May, because the Japanese Navy used the East Longitude date, and set their clocks on Tokyo time.) At once a supply and requisitioning force, 1400 strong, swung into action on her. Her hull was patched, her compartments braced with timbers, and a few of the watertight doors were made to close. The repairs were rough-and-ready and three of the boilers damaged in the Coral Sea battle were not even touched. For this reason *Yorktown* could only reach a top speed of 27 knots.

Nimitz had had another problem to resolve during this period of preparation. Admiral 'Bull' Halsey, the US Pacific Fleet's most aggressive carrier admiral, fell ill. He was worn out with the strain of months of combat patrol after Pearl Harbor. Nimitz's choice of a replacement was Rear Admiral Raymond Spruance, a cruiser task force commander, who was exactly the opposite of the flamboyant Halsey. Quiet, courageous and cautious, Spruance's un-assuming manner concealed a cool mind and sound judgment. In the days that were to come he was to justify Nimitz's confidence in him.

On the day that the giant *Yamato* sailed out of Hiroshima Bay with six other battleships behind her, Spruance sortied from Pearl Harbor, with *Hornet* and *Enterprise* screened by six cruisers and nine destroyers. This was Task Force 16. Twenty-four hours later *Yorktown* was pronounced ready for sea. Rear-Admiral 'Black Jack' Fletcher hoisted his flag in her again, and with two cruisers and five destroyers he too sailed from Pearl Harbor. This was Task Force 17, and like Task Force 16 it was on a course for Midway. On the island itself, the garrison watched and waited. Meanwhile, Yamamoto – unaware that his plans were known to the Americans – continued to believe that there would be little opposition to his invading force. According to his Intelligence there were 750 Marines, 24 flying boats, 12 bombers and 20 fighters on Midway, nothing much in the Aleutians, and little of military significance there apart from the US base installations at Dutch Harbor.

Yorktown and her escorts made contact with *Enterprise* and *Hornet* and their escorts shortly before noon on 2 June. Fletcher in *Yorktown* took command of the combined task forces and a course was then set for a point northeast of Midway.

Activity in and around Hiroshima Bay quickened as the cherry blossom faded during May 1942. Sixty-eight warships were anchored off Hashirajima. Among them were the seven great battleships *Yamato, Nagato, Mutsu, Ise, Hyuga, Fuso* and *Yamashiro* which the Navy Air Corps sarcastically referred to as 'The Hashira Fleet' because they had been at anchor since the beginning of the war, awaiting Yamamoto's 'one decisive surface battle.' Torpedo nets ringed these giants, for the

Far left: Rear Admiral Takeo Kurita commanded the Midway Occupation Force's Support Group.
Left: Vice-Admiral Raymond Spruance (right) took over direction of the battle when Fletcher's flagship was put out of action. He then became Chief of Staff to Nimitz (left).
Right: The Midway Occupation Force's Transport Group was under Rear Admiral Raizo Tanaka.
Below: Dauntless dive bombers crowd the after end of *Enterprise*'s flight deck. Astern are two oilers, two destroyers and USS *Hornet*.

Imperial Navy itself had demonstrated at Pearl Harbor what could happen to unprotected ships if they were attacked by torpedo bombers.

The harbor seethed with sea-borne traffic as ships plied between ships and shore, shuttling supplies. The weather was warm and summer was fast drawing on. The *Ryujo* and *Junyo*, the two carriers assigned to Vice-Admiral Hosogaya's Northern Force were loading heavy winter clothing. The Midway operation was still officially a secret, but it was not difficult for the sailors to guess that part of the huge armada would be operating in Arctic waters.

On 18 May Colonel Kiyinao Ichiki, who was to command the assault troops in the Midway landing, boarded the *Yamato* to be given the details of the operational plan. Ichiki was the last of the commanders to be briefed, and on 20 May the operation began to get under way. That day the transports carrying Ichiki's soldiers sailed from Yokosuka and Kure for Saipan. They arrived there four days later, to link up with Rear-Admiral Takeo Kurita's Support Force of heavy cruisers which arrived from Guam the same day. Part of Hosogaya's Northern Force also steamed out of the Inland Sea, heading for Ominato on northern Honshu, the staging point for the Aleutians invasion

The battleships and carriers which were to move directly to the battle area still had a week to wait, however, and Yamamoto decided to put the time to good use. On 21 May he led the Main Force, Kondo's Second Fleet and Nagumo's Carrier Strike Force out through the Bungo Strait into the open sea for two days fleet maneuvers – the biggest maneuvers since the outbreak of war, and the last ever to be staged in the open sea by the Japanese Imperial Navy.

When they arrived back in the Hashirajima Anchorage on 25 May, another rehearsal of the forthcoming operation was staged. Afterward Vice-Admiral Takagi, who had commanded the Japanese fleet in the Coral Sea battle, lectured the assembled officers on the forthcoming engagement. Lack of information and false reports led him to paint a much rosier picture of events than was actually true. He was certain that the *Yorktown* was so badly damaged – if not actually sunk – that she would be unable to take part in the operation. He could not know, of course, that emergency repairs would be effected at Pearl Harbor which would allow her to be ready in time.

The stage was now almost set for the battle, and on 27 May – Navy Day, when Japanese sailors celebrated Admiral Togo's victory over the Russians at Tsushima – Yamamoto invited all his senior officers to a farewell party aboard his flagship. The success of the operation was toasted in sake, drunk from cups presented to Yamamoto by the Emperor.

At 0800 hours next morning a signal flag was hoisted to the mast of Nagumo's flagship, the *Akagi*. As the *banzais* echoed round the harbor anchor chains rattled, and the unwieldy carriers and their escorting destroyers began to move. The order to sail had come at last, and the ships of Nagumo's Carrier Task Force were on their way to spearhead the Imperial Navy in its greatest battle ever.

When the carriers steamed out of anchorage it was a fine sunny day, and the crews of Yamamoto's battleships lined the rails to wave their caps and cheer as the ships of the Carrier Force passed. For their passage up the Bungo Channel the 21 ships formed a single column, with the light cruiser *Nagara* (Rear-Admiral Susumu Kimura) leading them. Behind the *Nagara* came Rear-Admiral Hiroaki's cruisers. With *Tone*, Hiroaki's flagship, and her sistership, the *Chikuma*, were the battleships *Haruna* and *Kirishima*. Behind *Kirishima* came the carriers *Akagi* and *Kaga* under Nagumo's direct command, with Rear-Admiral Yamaguchi's *Hiryu* and *Soryu* at the rear.

As they passed groups of fishing boats, their crews waved excitedly, and the sailors aboard the warships confidently returned their waves. All Japan was aware that this was the greatest armada ever seen in the Pacific and that its ships were about to take part in an enterprise which would change the history of Asia, if not of the world. The officers were less happy. Many of them were worried that news of the fleet's sailing might have leaked out. They felt that security had been slack, and people in Kure had guessed where they were making for. They would have been even more anxious if they had known that some of the ships had sent messages which had actually mentioned their destination. (One ship was asked where mail was to be directed, and confidently replied, 'Midway.')

Tension increased when the carriers entered the blue waters of the Pacific, where American submarines were known to be watching the progress of this formidable fleet. Nagumo knew his movements were being reported to Nimitz in Pearl Harbor because his radio operators were able to intercept the messages sent by US submarines. He was unable to stop the information getting through, but he himself was confident that Nimitz would not guess that the objective was Midway. The submarines did not attempt to attack the Japanese fleet; it was too powerful for them, and their first responsibility was simply to dog Nagumo and report his whereabouts. As the possibility of an attack always existed the Japanese armada adopted a circular formation when the shores of Japan became more distant. *Nagara* continued to lead the way, and behind her the four carriers were surrounded by two wide circles of screening ships, with 12 destroyers forming the outer circle. On board the ships, strict antisubmarine watches were maintained and planes patrolled overhead. As time passed and no submarines were sighted, tension gradually began to relax.

On 28 May, Hosagaya's Northern Force

and the Attu and Kiska Invasion Forces sailed from Ominato. Further south the transports carrying the troops for Midway also sailed, escorted by the cruiser *Jintsu* and 12 destroyers. In order to deceive any US submarines which might be lurking in the area, the invasion convoy set off on a westerly course and skirted round Tinian before heading for the east. Meanwhile Kurita's Support Group of heavy cruisers sailed from Guam on a parallel course some 40 miles southwest of the invasion convoy. Last to leave anchorage were the cruisers and the destroyers, the light carrier *Zuiho* of Vice-Admiral Kondo's Second Fleet and, finally, Yamamoto's battleships. Kondo's ships accompanied Yamamoto for the first two days of their voyage, before sailing away to rendezvous with Ichiki's transports, plowing slowly toward Midway.

Five months had elapsed since the Japanese battleships had left home waters. Since the beginning of the war they had been kept back in the Inland Sea, training for what most of the officers hoped would be a major role in the anticipated battle against the US Pacific Fleet. The sailors were tired of training now; morale was high and they were anxious to show their mettle. Like Nagumo however, Yamamoto and Kondo were nervous about submarines, and when Intelligence reported six enemy submarines operating in Japanese waters along the path and four more near Wake Island, antisubmarine precautions were intensified. Once the open sea was reached, the battleships formed up in two parallel columns – *Yamato, Nagato* and *Mutsu* on the right, and *Ise, Hyuga, Fuso* and *Yamashiro* on the left – surrounded by a circular screen of cruisers and destroyers. The carrier *Hosho* steamed between the two columns of battleships, launching and recovering a constant sequence of antisubmarine patrol planes. Zigzagging erratically every five to 10 minutes, the fleet steamed steadily southeast at a speed of 18 knots along the planned route.

Nobody knew better than Yamamoto the potential consequences of his lack of knowledge of the Pacific Fleet's movements. Two days after the gigantic fleet had left the Inland Sea, Lieutenant Tomano – the survivor of an ill-fated earlier flight to Midway – was told to make a full-moon reconnaissance of Pearl Harbor. Before he launched his attack, Yamamoto wanted to know how many of Nimitz's ships were still in their base. For this long range reconnaissance Tomano was to fly one of the new 31-ton four-engined Kawanishi flying boats. Without a bomb load this aircraft could fly 5000 miles without refuelling at a cruising speed of 160 knots. For the flight to Oahu it was proposed that Tomano's aircraft should be refuelled off French Frigate

Shoals near Midway by one of Yamamoto's I-Class submarines which was already making for the Shoals. From experience with a previous raid and their radio intercepts, the Americans knew that French Frigate Shoals were being used as a refuelling point, and when the Japanese submarine arrived there her lookout saw an American destroyer patrolling in the very area for which he was making. Her captain at once signalled that refuelling would be impossible, and, instead of telling the submarine to move to nearby Necker Island and refuel there, the Japanese Naval Staff in Tokyo cancelled Tomano's flight.

In the event, this was a stupid thing to do, for if Tomano had refuelled and flown on to Hawaii, he might well have sighted the *Yorktown* and *Lexington* Task Forces moving away from Pearl Harbor toward Midway. This at least would have given Yamamoto some prior warning as to the sort of opposition he was going to meet. As it was, Yamamoto sailed almost completely ignorant of the strength and position of the US carriers, and what little information the Japanese did glean was often lost through misunderstanding or inefficiency.

One signal from Tokyo tended to give weight to the theory that the US Pacific Fleet was in the South Pacific. The message said that there was a good deal of American fleet activity in the Solomons, suggesting the US carriers were still there. This seemed to indicate that Nimitz had not discovered the Japanese intentions, for Nagumo knew that were he aware of them, he would have recalled all his carriers to Pearl Harbor.

Nagumo's carriers did not have an easy voyage, and on 2 June they ran into a heavy sea mist which by dawn next morning had become an impenetrable blanket of fog. In his plotting room aboard the *Akagi* the commander of the Strike Force reviewed his plans. Despite the lack of information Nagumo felt reasonably confident that all was well, and he decided to go ahead with the attack on Midway as planned.

His carriers were still groping their way through the fog, and it was impossible to use visual signals – the only kind which could not possibly be intercepted. Owing to the full moon and the position of the troopships, Nagumo was tied to a strict schedule and consequently decided to risk using *Akagi*'s low-powered radio to send out an order to the fleet to change course toward Midway. If the Americans picked it up it would alert them and all surprise would be lost. He could only hope that such a low-powered transmission would be heard by his ships only. The flagship *Yamato* heard his message clearly and this was the only confirmation to reach Yamamoto that his carriers were going to attack as planned. Fortunately for Nagumo, the Americans on Midway did not pick up this vital message sent out just before the battle. Having taken the decision and made all his plans, Nagumo turned in to his bunk.

Above left: Mutsu was one of three battleships with the Main Body.
Left: The battleship *Hyuga* supported the diversionary Aleutians attack.

3. FIRST STRIKES

Far right: Vice-Admiral Frank Fletcher was the American tactical commander at the start of the Battle of Midway, but the disabling of his flagship *Yorktown* forced him to relinquish command to Spruance.
Left: A Japanese naval officer watches flight deck operations from the island of his carrier.
Below: American flight deck crews position a force of Dauntless dive bombers for takeoff.

The Battle of Midway opened at 0500 hours on 3 June 1942, more than 1000 miles north of the atoll itself, when aircraft from the carriers *Ryujo* and *Junyo* took off from a point south of Rat Island to strike at Dutch Harbor 250 miles east of the outermost edge of the Aleutian chain.

At Pearl Harbor Admiral Nimitz was not deceived by the reports of this attack. He knew that the main Japanese thrust was directed toward Midway, and he wanted to locate Yamamoto's armada as quickly as possible. The search for the Japanese ships began soon after 0400 hours on the morning of 3 June, when 23 Catalina flying boats rumbled down the runways at Midway. These slow and ugly parasol-winged amphibious reconnaissance aircraft were taking off on the mission for which Nimitz had intended them. The furthest limit of their searches was 700 miles, and with normal visibility of 25 miles, each could scan an eight-degree sector radiating from Midway. Thus the 23 PBYs were able to patrol a semicircle extending 700 miles from Midway. Any Japanese carrier which was going to attack at dawn must travel about that distance by nightfall. This would enable her to launch her planes before daylight next day – after steaming at top speed all night – at a point about 200 miles from the island.

Shortly after 0800 hours on the same morning, Ensign Jewell Reid of Kentucky was approaching the 700-mile limit of his patrol when he spotted something and immediately radioed back to Midway, 'Investigating suspicious vessels.' Half an hour later he reported sighting two cargo vessels, and soon afterward the 'main body, bearing 261, distance 700 miles from Midway. Six ships in column.' Below him Reid had seen Ichiki's invading force and Kondo's cruisers, but he was wrong in deducing this was Yamamoto's main body. The Main Force had not been spotted yet, nor had Nagumo's all-important carrier Task Force.

Reid continued to shadow Ichiki's transports and their escorts until 1100 hours, sending back a stream of radio reports. From there Nimitz deduced that there were 11 Japanese ships west of Midway, steaming toward the island at 19 knots. Nimitz decided that these ships were nothing to do with the carrier force he was hoping to find and he was right. It was not yet time to commit Fletcher's forces, but at 1230 hours nine B-17s took off from Midway to attack the convoy Reid had spotted. Four hours later they sighted a force of 'five battleships or heavy cruisers and about 40 others.' The Fortresses separated into three Vees and descended to 8000 feet. Extra fuel tanks in their bomb bays left room for only half a bomb load, four 600-pounders apiece but the bombardiers thought they hit a heavy cruiser and a transport. The Fortresses had not yet landed when four Catalinas with volunteer crews took off to make a night torpedo attack. Catalinas were not built to carry torpedoes, and their crews were not trained to drop them. Nevertheless three pilots managed to find the Japanese force. They approached from down-moon, so that the Japanese ships would be silhouetted, and one torpedo blew a hole in the tanker *Akebono Maru*. The weary crews then turned their airplanes back toward the dawn. They were almost home when they received messages that Midway was under attack.

Meanwhile, the two US Naval Task Forces had kept their position about 300 miles from Midway. Fletcher was certain that the carriers he was waiting for would approach Midway from the northwest, under cover of bad weather, and this was exactly what Nagumo's carriers were doing, as they sailed at top speed for Midway. As soon as the Japanese airplanes were committed to an attack on the island Fletcher hoped from his position on the flank to launch his own planes against their carriers. By 1930 hours on 3 June, with the Japanese attack on Midway expected to begin at dawn on 4 June, Nagumo's Carrier Strike Force had still not been located, and Nimitz was anxious. *Yorktown, Enterprise* and *Hornet*, together with their escorts, changed course to the southwest and headed toward Midway.

Aboard Nagumo's ships morale was rising as zero hour for their strike on Midway approached. According to Japanese intelligence the atoll was still guarded by only 750 troops and 60 planes. If this was the case Ichiki's force, 2800 strong and covered by 300 planes from the four carriers, ought to be able to overwhelm them easily.

At 1445 hours, when the Japanese carriers were about 250 miles northwest of Midway, the aircrews were ordered on deck. It was a dark, warm morning and as the pilots scrambled out of their bunks its silence was shattered by the roar of their planes' engines being warmed up. Nagumo himself briefed the *Akagi*'s pilots, ending his orders with the words, 'Although the enemy is lacking in fighting spirit, he will probably come out to attack during our invasion.' Despite this show of confidence, Nagumo was still inclined to be cautious. Only half his planes were sent to assault Midway and his best pilots had been held back to meet a possible American counter-attack. He was still convinced that there were no American carriers in the immediate vicinity, but – just in case there were – he decided to put up an air search. Japanese air patrols were usually very meticulous, but on this occasion the patrol was very casual – with dire results. According to the air plan, a plane from the *Akagi* was to fly south for 300 miles, then turn and fly 60 miles east; a *Kaga* plane was to fly the same pattern southeast. Two planes from each of the heavy cruisers *Tone* and *Chikuma* were to fly 300 miles, turn left and fly 60 miles, and then return. The last plane, from *Haruna*, was to fly only 150 miles, then turn left and fly 40 miles before returning.

Had it worked as planned, this search would have produced vital information, but it did not. The carriers *Akagi* and *Kaga* launched their planes on schedule at 1630 hours, but *Tone*'s two planes were delayed for 30 minutes by catapult trouble, and one of the planes from *Chikuma* developed engine trouble and was forced to turn back at 1835 hours. Most of the others ran into bad weather and returned halfway through their search.

Above: Japanese aircrew parade before a mission.
Above right: Two American sailors relax during a lull in the action aboard USS *Yorktown.*
Above far right: The Nakajima B5N 'Kate' was the standard IJN carrier-based torpedo bomber in the early war years.
Below right: The Douglas SBD Dauntless proved to be a highly successful warplane at Midway.
Below: A Kate pictured during its takeoff run.

The luck of war was clearly against the Japanese at this moment. If the *Chikuma* plane which developed engine trouble had been able to continue its search it would have flown directly over the American carriers and Nagumo would have been warned. Similarly, the late takeoff of *Tone*'s two planes was also unfortunate. Had they taken off on time instead of half an hour late, they too might have found the American carriers and given an early alarm.

Dawn still had not broken when the floodlights on the *Akagi*'s deck were switched on and the first bomber sped down the flight deck and roared off into the night. Other planes followed and as they took off there were cries of *banzai*! from the flagship's crew who had assembled on deck to witness what was supposed to be an historic moment. Similar scenes were

being enacted on the *Kaga*, *Hiryu* and *Soryu*. A slight southwest wind and a calm sea enabled the four carriers to hold course easily while the aircraft were taking off and within 15 minutes 108 planes were circling into formation above the fleet. It was 0445 hours on 4 June. The crucial battle for the control of the Pacific was about to begin.

At 0500 hours the Japanese planes were on course for Midway. Of the 108 planes, 36 were Zeros, 36 torpedo bombers (carrying bombs for the strike) and 36 were dive bombers. Lieutenant Joichi Tomonaga, the air ground commander from *Hiryu*, was their leader. This was his first battle in the Pacific, but he had flown operation missions in China as had Lieutenant Shoichi Ogawa commanding the dive bombers from *Akagi* and *Kaga*, and Lieutenant Masaharu Suganomai leading the Zeros.

Two hundred miles away from Nagumo's fleet, there was a great deal of activity. On board the *Yorktown*, 10 dive bombers were prepared for a search mission covering a 100-mile northern semicircle west to east. Almost at the same time 16 B-17s were taking off from Midway to look for and bomb the Japanese carriers, if they found them. The Catalinas had already taken off for their usual patrols. Thus, together with the reconnaissance planes, Tomonaga's strike force and the dive bombers for *Yorktown*, there were now 152 aircraft in the air from the two sides, and their pilots were all eager to begin the fight. This was the situation at 0520 hours when Nagumo signalled his ships to say that he would probably send a second assault wave against Midway soon after Tomonaga attacked.

Ten minutes later the *Akagi* was spotted by a Catalina which radioed back to Midway that it had a Japanese carrier in sight, bearing 320 degrees from the island, distance 150 miles. *Enterprise* intercepted the message and passed it to *Yorktown*. Nagumo's fleet was now speeding toward the island at 26 knots, but both Fletcher and Spruance knew approximately where he was. Minutes later a second Catalina radioed a message in clear, 'Many planes headed Midway, distance 150.' Tomonaga was halfway to the atoll. The alarm was sounded on Midway and every aircraft was ordered into the air, some to attack the Japanese carriers, some to intercept the incoming planes. By 0600 hours every airplane that could leave the ground was airborne.

Tomonaga's 36 Vals, 36 Kates and their escort of 36 Zeros hit Midway just before 0630 hours. They were met by 27 obsolescent Buffaloes, who had little hope of fending off the attack. They were not up against the famous Zero with its rounded wing tip which had proved such a success at the beginning of the Pacific war. This was a new, even more maneuverable aircraft with tapering wings – an improved version of the original Zero which was to become known by the Allies as the 'Hamp.' Not only were old Buffaloes inferior in performance, they were also outnumbered, and Lieutenant Suganomai easily prevented the inexperienced American pilots from reaching Tomonaga's bombers. Fifteen of the Buffaloes were shot down in the course of a brisk and lively action and of the 12 that survived, seven were so battered that they never flew again.

Meanwhile, Tomonaga's bombers were flying in to strike the sandy atoll. Commander Yahachi Tanabe, whose submarine, *I-168*, was prowling 10 miles south of Sand Island, had a first-class view of the bombing. 'The island,' he wrote after the war, 'turned into a mass of flames, with exploding fuel tanks and military buildings.

We saw it become covered with flames and thick, black smoke. I let my navigator, communications officer, gunnery officer and a few others take a turn looking through the periscope.' A cheer burst from the crew when Tanabe announced that a large fuel tank had exploded. In spite of heavy anti-aircraft fire, bombs fell on the island's power station, as well as on the fuel tanks. However, the antiaircraft fire daunted the Japanese pilots and for the most part the bombing was erratic.

US gunners had shot down 10 Japanese planes and they swore that if visibility had not been reduced by the smoke from the burning oil tank they would have shot down 10 more. Tomonaga realizing that the damage his bombers had inflicted was far from effective, radioed at 0700 hours that a second strike was necessary, but at 0707 hours another report assured Nagumo that Sand Island had been bombed and 'great results obtained.'

A second strike had already been prepared and another 108 planes, manned by Nagumo's best pilots, were drawn up on his carriers' decks. Nagumo knew that if he gave the order to launch this attack he would have little left to send against American surface ships if his scouts spotted any. As he paced the flag bridge of *Akagi*, pondering the risk, US planes appeared on the horizon. These were 10 torpedo-carrying Avengers and Fortresses from Midway. The Avengers attacked first, dropping their torpedoes from a low altitude and pressed their attack home with great courage. Several torpedoes foamed toward *Akagi* but she nimbly dodged three of them and the other carriers dodged the rest. Zeros then shot down five of the Avengers and two of the B-17s and only three planes of the original 10 got back to Midway. It had been a valiant effort, but was piecemeal and ineffective. However, one important result was that it disturbed the Japanese at a critical moment and delayed the launching of the second strike against Midway.

Nagumo finally reached his decision to hit Midway again and eliminate the possibility of more land-based attacks on his fleet at about 0715 hours. By this time his search planes had been gone for over two hours and should have reached a point 200 miles distant. Yet there had been no reports of any US ships or carriers. In such circumstances, Nagumo felt it was safe to assume there were no carriers near him, and sent the fateful order, 'Planes in the second wave stand by to carry out attack.' Then he added, 'Reload with bombs.'

This second instruction threw the decks of *Kaga* and *Akagi* into confusion. Each of the 2 carriers had 18 planes loaded with torpedoes, ready for takeoff in case an enemy surface fleet was sighted. Now all 36 planes had to be taken below, their torpedoes removed and bombs slung in their places. The planes then had to be brought up to the flight decks.

In retrospect these orders may appear as a colossal blunder on Nagumo's part, yet in the context of events it was clearly a reasonable decision. Midway obviously had to be struck again and the airfield there put out of action. Nagumo's ships had been attacked by land-based aircraft and at the time the decision was taken there was no evidence of any enemy surface fleet in the area where they could be expected. So, Nagumo reasoned that to launch another attack on Midway would be no gamble. Also the first group of planes would soon be back to replace those he was now about to dispatch. As soon as they landed they could be refuelled and rearmed, ready for any surface engagement when his air patrols found a US fleet. Viewed objectively, it was a logical decision.

While the maintenance crews were lowering the torpedo bombers to refit them with bombs, an excited message came in from the *Tone*'s plane, 'Have sighted an estimated 10 ships, bearing 010 degrees, 240 miles from Midway, heading southwest at more than 20 knots.' If what the pilot had seen was a carrier task force, this was disastrous news and Nagumo's immediate response was to send back a curt signal ordering the pilot to, 'ascertain what types.' Half an hour passed before a coherent reply was received and during that time Nagumo's thoughts were again interrupted by another attack by American bombers. First came 16 Dauntless dive bombers from Midway. Of these, eight were knocked out and the other

Below left: A formation of Dauntlesses flies over Midway
Below: A Grumman TBF-1 Avenger carries out a practice torpedo drop in 1942.

eight driven off by Zeros almost as soon as they went into their attack dives. They were followed by the 15 Fortresses which had headed westward at dawn in search of the Invasion Force and which had turned north when they had picked up the radio report of the position of Nagumo's carriers. At 20,000 feet they dropped their bombs on the four carriers and Nagumo logged, 'Enemy bombs: *Soryu*. No hits. *Akagi* and *Hiryu* also subjected to bombing.' Pilots of B-17s, watching their 500-pound bombs splashing nearly four miles below, were certain they had hit the carriers. Returning to base with empty bomb racks, they claimed three hits on two carriers. In fact all they had scored was a near-miss on the *Akagi*.

A reply from the *Tone*'s reconnaissance plane came at 0800 hours, 'Enemy have five cruisers and five destroyers.' When Nagumo read the message he was greatly relieved. About half an hour later he was staggered when another message from *Tone*'s second plane reported, 'Enemy force accompanied by what appears to be an aircraft carrier.' Identification was not long coming, 'Two additional enemy ships apparently cruisers sighted. Carrier believed to be *Yorktown* with group.'

It was almost 0830 hours and Tomonaga's planes, returning from the first attack on Midway, were beginning to arrive overhead. Nagumo now knew that he was up against a big American fleet with at least one carrier. A quick decision was imperative. He could either attack the US ships before he launched another strike against Midway, or else he could recover and rearm the aircraft that were overhead before he did anything else. Most of the returning fighters were nearly out of fuel and some of the planes were obviously in distress. If he did not allow them to land at once, planes and pilots would be lost in the sea. On the other hand, if he recovered these planes and rearmed them he would be as strong as he had been when he launched the first wave. Other problems also had to be solved. He could send his dive bombers immediately against the American ships and he could launch his torpedo bombers even though they were now armed with bombs and even though they would also have to attack without fighter cover.

If he ordered the bombers on deck to circle out of danger until enough fighters could land, refuel and take off again to provide escort, the planes which had returned from Midway would have to be kept in the air until the bombers had cleared the deck. Damaged planes would have to take their chance. If they were not able to keep on flying they would have to crash-land in the sea.

Ultimately more was to rest on his decision than the Battle of Midway alone, but it is doubtful if Nagumo realized this at the time he ordered the flight decks to be cleared and the first wave of aircraft to be brought in.

4. DISASTER FOR NAGUMO

It was a clear, sunny morning with a few high clouds when Nagumo took stock of the situation at about 0900 hours on 4 June 1942. As he gazed out from the bridge of the *Akagi* everything seemed satisfactory. The survivors of the attack from Midway had flown off in their shrapnel-torn machines, and there was not an American plane in sight. His own mighty carriers were unscathed. Tomonaga's fliers had reported leaving a trail of destruction at Midway, and it was clear that the Americans had lost a large proportion of their Midway-based aircraft. Nagumo thought that the Americans had attacked with all their force, and so far their attacks had been easily driven off. As he looked at his four great carriers it seemed that he had every reason for confidence.

At 0834 hours the *Tone*'s scout radioed that he was returning to his ship. He had been in the air since 0500 hours and he was almost out of fuel. At that time the carriers were under attack and 20 minutes elapsed before Nagumo had time to reply. Then the scout was curtly instructed to postpone his return and to, 'maintain contact with enemy until arrival of four relief planes. Go on the air with your long-wave transmitter.'

Nagumo now felt ready to deal with the new menace, and he radioed Yamamoto, 'Enemy composed of one carrier, five cruisers, five destroyers sighted 240 miles from Midway. We are heading for it.' At the same time the blinker on the *Akagi* signalled his captains, 'After homing operations proceed northward. We plan to contact and destroy the enemy task force.' Ten minutes later, when the last Zero to return from Midway had landed on her deck, the *Akagi* turned and signalled for maximum battle speed. Soon the ships were shuddering as Nagumo's fleet speeded up to 30 knots. Aboard the four carriers the planes were being refuelled and rearmed; above them 18 fighters circled in a constant protective patrol.

By 0918 hours most of the Japanese torpedo planes had been rearmed and were ready for takeoff. On the lower decks the maintenance crews waited beside the heavy bombs they had changed for torpedoes. There had not been sufficient time to lower the bombs into the magazines, so they had been carelessly stacked around the carriers. On their flight decks *Akagi* and *Kaga* each had three fighters and 21 torpedo planes ready for takeoff, while *Hiryu* and *Soryu* each had three fighters and 18 torpedo planes ready.

The signal for them to take off was just about to be given, when there was a shout from the ship's lookout, who had spotted 15 American planes heading toward them low over the water. There was a frantic scurry as the Japanese fliers and deck crews tried to get their machines off the decks, and as the American attack started the Zeros swung into the air. Meanwhile the *Akagi*'s radio was buzzing with reports that more groups of American aircraft were heading toward the carriers. Both Nagumo and Captain Aoki on the bridge of the *Akagi* were perplexed and alarmed. There were more planes than could have been launched from a single carrier, and Nagumo ordered the *Soryu* to launch her scout plane to try to find out how many US carriers there actually were.

Dawn on 4 June had found the American fleet about 220 miles northeast of Midway. A four-knot breeze blew from the southeast, clouds were low and broken and visibility was about 12 miles. Fletcher's Task Force 17 with the carrier *Yorktown*, was steaming 10 miles to the north of Spruance's Task Force 16, with the carriers *Enterprise* and *Hornet*. Scout planes from the *Yorktown* had been in the air since before dawn, searching the sector northwest of Midway. It was not until 0603 hours that Fletcher got the message he had been waiting for, 'Two carriers and battleships,' together with their bearing, distance, course and speed. Reports that the Japanese were bombing the atoll flowed in while this data was being laid out and assessed on the plotting board.

The Japanese carriers were too far to be reached with an immediate strike. However, if Nagumo held his course – it was probable that he would be able to do so because a head wind would help the launching and recovering of his planes – an intercepting course would soon bring him within range of the Americans. At 0607 hours Fletcher ordered Spruance to, 'Proceed southwesterly and attack enemy carriers when definitely located. I will follow as soon as my planes are recovered.'

Spruance steamed ahead at 25 knots with *Enterprise* and *Hornet* and by 0700 hours the range had closed to within striking distance of his torpedo bombers. The two American carriers now separated, dividing the screening vessels between them. Finally, the carriers turned into the wind, and the first plane roared down the *Enterprise*'s deck. Nearly 150 miles away Midway's first Marine planes had begun their assault on the Japanese carriers, as 57 planes – 10 Wildcat fighters, 33 Dauntless dive bombers, and 14 Devastator torpedo bombers – from the *Enterprise* formed up. Nearby the *Hornet* had launched an almost identical group of planes, 10 Wildcats, 35 Dauntless dive bombers, and 15 Devastators. Each group was ordered to attack one of the carriers now estimated to be 155

Right: Aichi D3A 'Val' dive bombers, their engines running, await their turn to takeoff.
Below right: Douglas TBD Devastator torpedo bombers are pictured aboard USS *Enterprise.*

miles southwest. By 0806 hours the launch was completed, the carriers swung out of the wind and their squadrons sped away.

Meanwhile the *Yorktown* had recovered her planes from the morning search and had turned to steam after Spruance. Fletcher knew from his code intercepts that he could expect to meet four or five Japanese carriers and when the scout planes reported only two he hesitated to commit all his resources. By 0830 hours, however, he decided he could not afford to miss the target which had been offered to him. Half of *Yorktown*'s aircraft – six Wildcats, 17 Dauntlesses and 12 Devastators – were launched for a follow-up strike. The re-

mainder of the *Yorktown*'s strength was kept in reserve, and more search planes were sent to look for the rest of Yamamoto's carriers.

Fifty minutes after *Yorktown*'s planes took off to join the battle, the first wave of aircraft from *Enterprise* and *Hornet* spotted two big columns of smoke just beyond the horizon. They had found Nagumo, and the first all-out clash between American and Japanese carrier fleets, for which the Coral Sea had been only a curtain-raiser, was about to begin.

The Japanese carrier force was a long way from its predicted position – it had maneuvered radically to dodge the planes from Midway, and had then turned northeast to attack Spruance. However, *Hornet*'s strike force Commander, Lieutenant Commander John Waldron, had flown a course straight for it. He had lost his fighters en route but was accompanied by his torpedo bombers. The *Hornet*'s fliers counted three carriers, six cruisers and 10 destroyers. He radioed back that the carriers' decks were loaded with planes, apparently being re-fuelled and rearmed, and that one of the carriers was definitely the *Soryu*. The message ended with the statement that he was going to attack. Apart from instructions to the squadron following him these were his last words.

To the lookouts on Nagumo's carriers, Waldron's torpedo bombers first appeared as tiny black specks on the horizon off *Akagi*'s starboard bow. When Waldron wiggled his wings as signal to start the attack, he was still eight miles from Nagumo's fleet. It was then that the Zeros circling high above plunged down on them and the rattle of the American rear gunners' machine-gun fire was punctuated by the louder, slower thump-thump of the Japanese fighters' cannon. As they came within range the antiaircraft guns aboard the cruisers and destroyers opened fire, and the carriers began to twist and turn in an effort to avoid the inevitable torpedoes. The antiaircraft fire was almost thick enough to screen the twisting ships. It gored huge holes in wings and fuselages, cut cables, smashed instruments and killed pilots and gunners. Plane after torn plane – 14 of them – plunged into the sea, burned briefly, and sank. A rear gunner in another squadron, miles away, overheard Waldron's last words, 'Watch those fighters! My two wingmen are going in the water.'

Except for the voice of the sole survivor, Ensign George Gay, nothing more was heard of the *Hornet*'s torpedo bombers. Gay heard Waldron and he heard his own gunner cry, 'They got me!' Then he was hit himself, twice, in the left hand and arm. His own target was the *Kaga*. He dropped his torpedo and flew down her flank, close to the bridge, where he could, 'see the little Jap captain jumping up and down and raising hell.'

A 20mm shell exploded on Gay's left rudder pedal, wounding him in the foot and smashing his controls, and his plane crashed between the *Kaga* and the *Akagi*. He swam back to get his gunner, but strafing Zeros made him dive and dive again and the gunner sank with the plane. A black cushion and a rubber raft floated to the surface. Gay was afraid to inflate the raft as it might draw the Zeros. So he put the cushion over his head and hid under it until twilight, with a hazardous grandstand view of the great battle that raged all day. Gay, still alive, was picked up by a Catalina at 1430 hours the next day. Waldron had launched a suicidal attack. Yet if it had not been for the gallant action of these pilots Nagumo's planes would have had time to take off, and they could have reversed the tide of the battle.

Fifteen minutes after *Hornet*'s torpedo bombers, *Enterprise*'s torpedo planes arrived, followed by *Yorktown*'s. Like Waldron's squadron they were without fighter protection, which was still circling uselessly 20,000 feet above them.

Excitement was at its height on the Japanese carriers as the planes swooped down to launch their torpedoes. Waves of low-level Devastators lumbered in through the antiaircraft fire and as they battled to break through the curtain of shellfire, the Zeros followed them to within a few feet of the water, trying to shoot them down before they could reach the veering carriers. The second wave registered no hits on the fast and expertly-handled Japanese carriers. The mission was also virtually suicidal. Of the 41 torpedo planes that had taken off only six returned safely but the Devastators made a sacrifice more effective than they knew. When, in the heat of the battle, they drew the deadly Japanese fighters down to sea level the Japanese carriers were left wide open to attack. While fighting off the torpedo bombers, the Japanese forgot to look up. Hidden in the high clouds following the torpedo planes were the US dive bombers.

The *Hornet*'s torpedo bombers could not find Nagumo. An American scout plane had radioed accurately the Japanese position but, after this report was received, Nagumo changed course, and the Japanese were not where the Americans expected to find them. *Hornet*'s 35 dive bombers continued on a false course until their fuel ran low. Then 21 returned to the carrier, and the remaining fourteen headed for Midway, where three crashed. Their accompanying fighters, with their shorter range, crash-landed in the sea when their fuel was exhausted.

Enterprise's dive bombers also failed to find the Japanese in the position given to them. They searched the area but the ocean was calm – and deserted. There was not a Japanese ship in sight and the Squadron Leader, Lieutenant Commander Clarence McClusky, had to decide whether his information was incorrect or whether Nagumo had changed course. The narrow margin of luck by which great battles are decided now

began to turn slightly toward the Americans. McClusky decided the Japanese carriers must have changed course and turned northward.

When McClusky gave the signal to turn north it was not only a lucky but a courageous decision, for his planes had already used up half their fuel. If they could not find the Japanese carriers quickly they would not be able to return. Just after 1000 hours – 25 minutes after he gave the change-course order – McClusky saw a faint white streak below him. It was the wake of a Japanese destroyer. Then three long vessels slid from under the broken cloud. Tiny flames and little dots all around them showed they were under attack. McClusky peered out of his cockpit and identified *Soryu* in the lead with *Kaga* and *Akagi* behind; he did not see *Hiryu* in the rear because she was still obscured by cloud.

Aboard the Japanese carriers the smoke was beginning to clear as the last torpedo plane staggered away, chased by Zeros, its crew exhausted by the fierce action. Nagumo had every reason to be pleased with the brisk morning's work. Wave after wave of American planes of all types had been beaten off without his carriers suffering any damage. All his aircraft were refuelled and equipped with armor-piercing bombs and torpedoes. He gave orders to launch them, and their engines began to roar as the four big Japanese carriers turned into the wind.

The first Zero was just leaving *Akagi*'s deck when a lookout shrieked a warning. With the guardian Zero still at wave-top height chasing off the last of the torpedo bombers, three of McClusky's planes screamed down on the *Akagi*. Other planes plunged down on the *Kaga*. This was the beginning of the end of Nagumo's carriers. With no radar to warn him of their approach and no fighters in a position to head them off, he was taken completely by surprise.

Only a couple of machine gunners recovered quickly enough to fire a few quick bursts at the Americans as the Japanese aircraft attempted to get clear of the carriers. It had little effect. As the American Dauntlesses pulled out of their whistling dives, their bombs were detached from their wings. Aboard the *Akagi* there was a blinding flash and two loud explosions. The guns stuttered into silence, their crews shocked or wounded, and when the thick black smoke cleared the American airplanes were nowhere in sight.

Peering through the smoke, Nagumo and his officers saw a fearful sight. The *Akagi* had received two direct hits. One had blown a huge hole in her flight deck and the other had wrenched and twisted the amidship elevator. The air was filled with burning splinters and the odour of petrol and hot metal. Charred, smoking corpses lay strewn over her deck. Then bombs that had been left lying on deck after the

Above, left and below left: The Mitsubishi A6M 'Zero' was the Imperial Japanese Navy's principal fighter aircraft, operating both from carriers and shore bases.
Below: The carrier *Kaga* takes violent evasive action to escape the bombs of Midway-based B-17s.

Left: Hiryu is straddled by the bombs of Boeing B-17s from the USAAF's 431st Bomb Squadron.
Right: A map traces the course of the Battle of Midway. At no time were the opposing ships in sight of each other.
Below: Captured Mitsubishi A6M Zero fighters are shipped to the United States for evaluation.

hasty reloading began to explode, shaking the bridge where Nagumo stood with his Chief of Staff, Admiral Kusaka, and Captain Aoki, *Akagi*'s commander.

Thick smoke made it difficult for them to see and the air was hot with yellow flames. As the fire licked along the flight deck more torpedoes and bombs began to explode and sailors fled from their fire-fighting apparatus half blinded. Spreading flames began to sear the bridge, their heat and smoke making it uninhabitable. Through the blackness Nagumo could see something worse – two glowing red smudges where *Kaga* and *Soryu* were supposed to be. He knew then that they too had been hit.

Kaga, Akagi's sister ship, was hit by McClusky's planes almost at the same time as *Akagi*. On her flight deck she had 30 planes, all armed and fuelled awaiting the signal to take off when the American dive bombers shot out of the clouds. McClusky's planes were too busy diving in their quick attack and getaway to know what was happening aboard the other carriers. At the same time as they struck the *Kaga* and the *Akagi*, the dive bombers from the carrier *Yorktown* hit *Soryu*.

Yorktown's planes had been launched more than an hour later than those with McClusky. When they did take off the weather was clearing rapidly. This helped them to find Nagumo easily, and consequently their attack followed immediately after that of McClusky. When they came out of the cloud, McClusky's planes were diving on *Akagi* and *Kaga*, so *Yorktown*'s planes concentrated on the third undamaged carrier, *Soryu*.

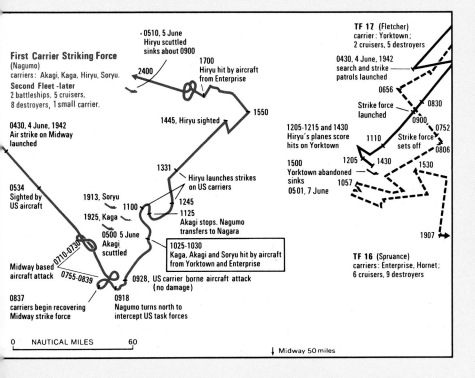

First Carrier Striking Force
(Nagumo)
carriers: Akagi, Kaga, Hiryu, Soryu.
Second Fleet -later
2 battleships, 5 cruisers,
8 destroyers, 1 small carrier.

0430, 4 June, 1942
Air strike on Midway
launched

0534
Sighted by
US aircraft

1913, Soryu
1925, Kaga

0500 5 June
Akagi
scuttled

Midway based
aircraft attack
0710-0730
0755-0839

0837
carriers begin recovering
Midway strike force

0918
Nagumo turns north to
intercept US task forces

0928, US carrier borne aircraft attack
(no damage)

1025-1030
Kaga, Akagi and Soryu hit by aircraft
from Yorktown and Enterprise

1245
1125
Akagi stops. Nagumo
transfers to Nagara

1100
1331
Hiryu launches strikes
on US carriers

1445, Hiryu sighted
1550
2400
1700
Hiryu hit by aircraft
from Enterprise

0510, 5 June
Hiryu scuttled
sinks about 0900

TF 17 (Fletcher)
carrier: Yorktown;
2 cruisers, 5 destroyers

0430, 4 June, 1942
search and strike
patrols launched

0656
0830
Strike force
launched
0900
0752
1110
0806
Strike force
sets off

1205-1215 and 1430
Hiryu's planes score
hits on Yorktown

1500
Yorktown abandoned
sinks
0501, 7 June

1205
1430
1057
1530

1907

TF 16 (Spruance)
carriers: Enterprise, Hornet;
6 cruisers, 9 destroyers

0 NAUTICAL MILES 60

Midway 50 miles

received this message Aoki decided there was only one course open to him, and he lashed himself to one of Akagi's anchors to await the end. Like most of the senior officers Aoki was intent on hari-kiri. Moreover he never got over the feeling that he ought to have stayed aboard and ultimately gone down with his ship. In the event he was persuaded by his silver-tongued navigator Commander Miura that he would be more useful alive than dead, and he was transferred to the destroyer Nowake.

The Kaga had suffered even more damage than the Akagi from four direct hits by 500-pound bombs. One which had landed near the bridge had killed everyone on it – including the ship's commander, Captain Jisaku Okada. The Flight Officer, Commander Takahisa Amagai, immediately took over the carrier, but the helmsman, blinded by a bomb flash, could not control her. Shattered glass on the bridge and smoke from bomb damage reduced visibility to zero, but the ship's position was far from hopeless, and Amagai ordered the crew to start clearing the decks and fighting the fires. Just as the fires were beginning to be brought under control, a small truck filled with gasoline for fuelling the planes blew up on the flight deck. Flames spread rapidly and when they began to lick the whole length of the carrier, Amagai was forced off the bridge. The damage-control crew whom he had organized fought desperately to halt the spreading flames. Realizing the end was near, Amagai ordered the Emperor's portrait to be lowered reverently down to the destroyer Hagikaze.

Some three-and-a-half hours after the dive-bombing attack, Amagai was still in command of the blazing Kaga when a new menace appeared. About half a mile from the carrier the telltale periscope of a submarine suddenly showed. The American submarine Nautilus, commanded by Lieutenant Commander William Brockman, which had been patiently stalking Nagumo's fleet, had seen an opportunity to strike a blow.

Minutes later, soon after 1400 hours, Lieutenant Commander Yoshio Kunisada, standing on the Kaga's listing deck, saw three white torpedo wakes streaking toward the starboard side of the carrier. There was nothing anyone could do but wait for the explosion. Disabled as she was, the Kaga could not swerve to dodge the torpedoes. The destroyers Hagikaze and Maikaze raced up to where the Nautilus had been spotted, and there was a series of dull booms as a pattern of depth charges was dropped round the crash-diving submarine. Miraculously, two of the torpedoes missed, and although the third struck it failed to explode. Instead of blowing a hole in the side of the flame-wracked carrier it turned out to be a lifesaver. Several sailors who had jumped or been blown overboard grabbed a floating section of the torpedo and clung to it until they were picked up by the destroyers' boats.

When she saw what had happened to her flagship, the destroyer Nowake came alongside to help with the fire fighting. Kusaka urged Nagumo to board her. The admiral, his face blackened with smoke, his eyes bloodshot, refused to leave his flagship. Captain Aoki pleaded with him, but as he spoke there were more explosions and the companionway to the bridge crashed in flames. Now the only means of escape was by rope from the bridge window.

Nagumo, realizing that the fires were out of control and that he could no longer direct the battle from the blazing carrier, climbed through the window. Helped by his flag lieutenant, Lieutenant Commander Nishibayashi, he swung down an already smoldering rope to one of Nowake's boats alongside. The time was 1046 hours, only 12 minutes since McClusky's first bomber had come plummeting like a sparrow hawk out of the clouds. As Nagumo left, the blast of explosions reverberated every few seconds, the metal companionways between decks were red hot, and half-choked sailors were beginning to jump overboard.

By this time Akagi was not answering her rudder and there was no response from the engine room. Then the ship stopped, with her bows still pointing into the wind as though she was getting ready to launch planes which were burning and exploding on her deck. The dynamos died and the lights went out and without electricity the fire pumps could no longer operate. Fire-fighting parties, wearing masks, rolled hoses down to the burning lower decks. As they staggered over the charred corpses of their comrades, explosions every few seconds wounded or killed more of them. Doctors and medical orderlies worked in suffocating heat and blinding smoke. The

clothing of wounded men began to smolder as they lay on deck. The lucky ones were strapped to bamboo stretchers and lowered over the side. Although fire had cut off the signal tubes to the bridge the engine rooms below were still undamaged, but the smoke filtering through the intakes made stokers gasp and clutch at their throats. Finally Commander Tampo, Akagi's chief engineer, clambered up a red-hot ladder and staggered through flames and smoke to the bridge to tell Captain Aoki that his men were dying. Aoki gave the order for all engineroom crew to come on deck and an orderly slid down a burning rope and ran along the smoke blackened decks to tell them. He never returned, and no one escaped from the engine room.

By this time all of Akagi's planes were either burning or had blown up, and the last of the aircrews were transferred to the destroyers. At 1615 hours Commander Tampo reported to the captain that there was no possibility of the ship steaming under her own power and as the last of the wounded were carried into the boats, the giant carrier was blazing from stem to stern. Finally Captain Aoki gave the order to abandon ship.

Aoki was the last man to leave the stricken vessel and it was 1920 hours when he was persuaded to board the launch from the destroyer Nowake. He had sent a message to Nagumo asking for permission to scuttle the Akagi. Nagumo never answered, but Yamamoto did, sending a brief order not to sink the ship. Yamamoto hated the idea of scuttling a vessel of the Imperial Navy, but his decision was determined also by his sentimental attachment to the ship. He had served many years on the Akagi and she was a great favorite of his. He was determined to tow her back if he could. When he

Above: The *Ise* served with the Aleutian Support Force but after Midway became a carrier/battleship.

By the late afternoon it was clear that the blazing unmanageable hulk of the *Kaga* was doomed, and at 1640 hours Amagai gave the order to abandon ship. Two hours later it seemed that the fire had died down and, in the hope of saving his old ship, Amagai led a fire-fighting party back. When the men eventually got aboard they were driven back by the heat. No one could stand on the red-hot decks and Amagai was reluctantly compelled to order his party to return to the destroyer which had brought them. They got away just in time; soon afterward two mighty explosions ripped *Kaga*'s hull and she rolled over to sink in a hiss of steam. Eight hundred men, more than a third of her crew, died with her.

On board the *Soryu*, the third target of the American dive-bombing attack, the devastation had been almost as great as aboard *Kaga*. Thirteen US dive bombers had plummeted down on the *Soryu* while those on her bridge were watching bombs falling on the *Kaga*. Three bombs struck the ship in quick succession and in next

to no time the whole of the flight deck was blazing. There may have been other hits too, but amid the noise and thump of exploding ammunition stacked on the deck it was hard to tell. Everything happened so quickly that most of those on the *Soryu* had little or no warning. Ten minutes afterward the engines stopped and the *Soryu*'s rudder failed to answer. Then a tremendous explosion below decks blasted many of the crew into the water. Other sailors jumped overboard as flames began to scorch their clothes. The destroyers *Hamaka* and *Isokaze*, circling round the blazing carrier, picked up as many as they could.

Captain Ryusaku Yanagimoto, *Soryu*'s commander fought to get the *Soryu* under control. The whole ship was ablaze from stem to stern and with constant explosions wracking her, he saw that there was no hope of saving her. Reluctantly he gave the order to abandon ship. He himself was determined to comply with the tradition and go down with her, and he remained on the bridge. However, no officer in the Imperial Navy was more popular than Yanagimoto, and his men were determined that he should not commit hari-kiri.

Before they slid down the ropes to the

waiting destroyers the biggest among them a navy wrestling champion, Chief Petty Officer Abe, was sent to reason with him. Abe was to drag the captain to safety by force if necessary. When Abe climbed up to *Soryu*'s bridge, Yanagimoto was standing sword in hand, silhouetted against the roaring flames, and the sight unnerved the petty officer. Saluting, Abe said, 'Captain I've come to take you to safety. The men are waiting, please come with me.' Yanagimoto did not reply. The stern look on his face was enough to deter Abe from laying hands on his skipper and he turned around and returned from the carrier in tears, and alone.

As the minutes ticked away the *Soryu* foundered lower and lower in the water. On the destroyer *Makigumo* standing by someone began singing the Japanese national anthem *Kimigayo*. Others took it up and some say that they could hear Yanagimoto's voice singing it with them on the bridge of the dying carrier. At 1913 hours with the strains of the song still ringing out over the water, the *Soryu*'s stern dipped and her bow rose high. For a moment, the ship paused, then settled down and was gone.

5. THE END OF YORKTOWN & HIRYU

When Nagumo left the blazing *Akagi* he transferred his flag to the light cruiser *Nagara*. Three of his carriers were already burning, and only the *Hiryu* remained to him as a strike weapon. He was worried about his lack of information on the number of American carriers opposing him, for there had been no report from the *Soryu*'s scout plane. This was sheer bad luck, for the *Soryu*'s plane had located and identified the three US carriers but had been unable to report back because of a faulty radio. Fortunately for Nagumo *Hiryu* was the flagship of Rear Admiral Tamon Yamaguchi, who appreciated the vital need for information.

Yamaguchi was one of the most able of the Imperial Navy's senior officers – certainly a more resolute and clear-thinking commander than Nagumo. As soon as the extent of the disaster that had struck Nagumo's force became clear to Yamaguchi he assumed responsibility for the operations and wasted no time in launching an attack on Fletcher's fleet. He decided that the number of American carriers was immaterial, and at 1040 hours Lieutenant Michio Kobayashi – an experienced pilot who had taken part in the Pearl Harbor raid – was ordered to take off with 18 Val dive bombers and an escort of six Zeros.

At this time *Yorktown*'s planes which had

sunk *Hiryu*'s sister carrier, *Soryu*, were winging their way home. At 1200 hours *Yorktown* was getting ready to recover the bombers and refuel her fighters when her radar picked up Kobayashi's planes, which were then 50 miles away. Refuelling was hastily abandoned, planes on the flight deck were quickly launched with orders to clear off out of trouble, and the returning bombers were waved away. A cruiser steamed up to either bow to add firepower

Below: Grumman F4F Wildcat fighters fly in echelon formation. Wildcats escorted the American carrier strike forces and performed defensive patrols.

Below: Yorktown, blazing amidships, lies dead in the water after the initial Japanese attack.

Above right: Naval antiaircraft guns took a toll of attacking aircraft.
Above: The scene on Yorktown's flight deck after the attack.

Right: The second Japanese bomb to hit Yorktown struck between her funnel and mast, the blast extinguished the fires in five out of her six boilers.

to *Yorktown*'s defenses, and fighters from the *Enterprise* and *Hornet* flew in to support her defensive umbrella – making a total of 28 Wildcats.

Kobayashi approached his target at 18,000 feet, and from about five miles distance he could see the American torpedo bombers, who were returning from their attack on his own fleet, circling to land on the US carrier. Clearly here was a bonus to his own strike and as he gave the signal to descend to 10,000 feet for the run in, he waved his Zero escort forward. They dived on the American bombers, chased by Wildcats, and in the fight which followed two Zeros were lost.

Other Wildcats now tore into the Japanese bombers in an effort to break up their formation, and the antiaircraft guns of the carrier and cruisers opened fire to put a curtain of steel above the *Yorktown*. Ten of Kobayashi's planes were shot down by the American Wildcats. There were not enough American fighters to stop some of the dive bombers getting through. Two more were disabled as they tried to pierce the shrapnel curtain, while another dropped his bomb harmlessly into the water and then crashed after it. Five of Kobayashi's original 18 planes survived and that was enough. Three bombs landed on *Yorktown*. One went straight down the smokestack into the engine room – knocking out all the boilers except one, and so effectively stopping the ship. The second exploded on the flight deck, blowing a big hole in it, and the third exploded near an ammunition magazine and a compartment of high-octane gasoline, which was hastily flooded with sea water to prevent fire.

Meanwhile *Soryu*'s scout plane had returned while Kobayashi's fliers were bombing *Yorktown* to find its home base blazing from end to end. So the pilot landed on *Hiryu* and reported to Rear Admiral Yamaguchi that the Americans actually had three carriers in action, *Enterprise*, *Hornet* and *Yorktown*.

This startling information forced Yamaguchi to make a quick reappraisal of the situation. *Hiryu* alone was now facing three enemy carriers, only one of which might have been knocked out in Kobayashi's attack. Clearly there was no time to be wasted, and he decided to strike quickly at the US carriers with every plane he could muster – a total of 10 torpedo bombers and six fighters.

Lieutenant Joichi Tomonaga, the officer who had led the assault on Midway, was chosen to lead the strike. There had not been enough time to repair his plane's fuel tank, damaged by gunfire over Midway, so he knew before he took off that he was flying a one-way mission.

At 1245 hours 16 planes took off from *Hiryu* and headed for the US carriers. En route they passed a forlorn little group of five Japanese planes flying in the reverse direction. They were all that was left of Kobayashi's strike.

When these five pilots landed on *Hiryu* they reported that six bombs had been dropped on an American carrier, that she could not move and was sending up great columns of smoke. Yamaguchi rightly concluded that this carrier must have been hit by at least two bombs and severely damaged. What he did not know was that damage-control parties in the *Yorktown* worked so effectively that in less than two hours – by 1400 hours – the carrier was again able to make 18 knots under her own power.

In consequence she was steaming along refuelling the rest of her fighters when at about 1430 hours her radar began tracking Tomonaga's torpedo group 40 miles away. Once more refuelling was suspended and the combat air patrol scrambled into the air. So speedily had *Yorktown*'s repairs been effected that when Tomonaga sighted an American carrier surrounded by escort ships he thought she was another un-damaged carrier; he could not believe it was *Yorktown*.

As his orders were to attack undamaged carriers, he signalled the order to do so and the bomber formation bifurcated. Tomonaga led one line, his second-in-command, Toshio Hashimoto, led the other. When they went into their dive *Yorktown* was still trying to get the rest of her planes into the air.

As before, Wildcats managed to shoot down some of the Japanese planes before they got within range of the ship's guns, and the barrage deterred others. A few of the determined Japanese succeeded in getting through – one of whom was Tomonaga. Signalling his pilots to follow him, he dived his yellow-tailed plane straight through the antiaircraft fire to launch his torpedoes. Then, knowing he could never get back, he crashed his plane on *Yorktown*, where it blew up in a sheet of flame. A long, dark smudge of brown smoke on *Yorktown*'s deck marked his pyre.

Inspired by Tomonaga's example other pilots followed him through the barrage to launch their torpedoes. Two struck amidships, less than 60 feet apart on the port side. As Hashimoto turned from his attack thick yellow smoke belched from the carrier and her 20,000-ton hull gave a great shudder and stopped dead in the water. 'She seemed to leap out of the water,' said an American sailor, 'then she sank back, all life gone.' It was 1445 hours and Hashimoto radioed back to the *Hiryu*, 'Two torpedo hits on the carrier. Believed to be of the *Yorktown* Class.'

This second raid was the last Japanese attack against American ships in the Battle of Midway. Only five torpedo bombers and three fighters, half the number launched, got back to *Hiryu*. They landed at 1830 hours and gave Yamaguchi details of their attack, claiming one carrier severely damaged. This, with the previous attack on *Yorktown* made him think that two American carriers were mortally hurt. He had no

Above: A 'Kate' breaks away from USS *Yorktown* after making its torpedo run.
Right: An attacking aircraft plunges blazing into the sea.
Below right: Dauntlesses position themselves for the dive onto the target.
Below: A curtain of antiaircraft fire greets Japanese torpedo aircraft attacking the American carrier task forces.

idea it was *Yorktown* his pilots had struck again. Even if he realized the situation there was nothing he could do to stave off the retribution that was now on its way.

At the same time as the survivors of Tomonaga's strike turned for home, the pilot of one of the *Yorktown*'s scout planes radioed to his own burning carrier. He had been searching the Pacific for three hours and had at last found Yamaguchi's *Hiryu*. His message gave its position as 100 miles away, and when Fletcher read it he decided that with dusk approaching an all-out strike was called for. At 1600 hours *Enterprise* began launching 24 Dauntless – 14 of which were refugees who had been unable to land on *Yorktown*. *Hornet* also launched 16 and the combined force set off without fighter escort because Fletcher, worried by the repeated attacks on his carriers, wanted his Wildcats to protect them against any more bombers. When the Dauntlesses had been flying for an hour they saw three curling towers of smoke silhouetted against the reddening sky. These marked the hulks of the *Kaga* and *Soryu* and the still burning *Akagi*. Swinging northward they now saw the rest of the Japanese fleet in a tight circle round their only surviving carrier, *Hiryu*.

Aircraft from *Hiryu* had made three attacks at dawn, including the one on Midway, and their number was sadly depleted. At 1630 hours, when the last of the ill-fated Tomonaga group was returning from *Yorktown*, they had been reduced to six fighters, five dive bombers and four torpedo bombers. Aircrew and sailors alike were exhausted, for in addition to their own attacks, 79 planes had attacked *Hiryu* since sunrise, and she had been kept busy dodging 26 torpedoes, and 70 bombs.

Yamaguchi, aggressive and desperate, was determined to salvage Yamamoto's operation, destroy the American carriers, and pluck victory from the jaws of defeat. He had decided to make a last attempt at dusk, when the uncertain light would give his few remaining planes a better chance to make a surprise attack on the Americans. This tactic had been tried without success in the Battle of the Coral Sea but Yamaguchi decided that he had no alternative but to risk it again.

At five o'clock – half an hour after Tomonaga's last plane landed – sweet rice-balls were served to the hungry, exhausted crew of the *Hiryu*. A handful of them had just finished refuelling the pitifully few planes for Yamaguchi's twilight attack, and the rest were hastily eating the rice as the carrier was turned into the wind to begin launching. Suddenly *Enterprise*'s bombers dived out of the sun. *Hiryu* had no radar, and once again there had been no long-range warning of their approach. Her commander, Captain Tomeo Kaku, swung the ship to starboard as the bombers came down and the Americans lost three planes to antiaircraft fire and Zeros. *Hiryu* twisted like a giant eel, but more American planes dived through the barrage, and four bombs exploded simultaneously on her deck.

One, bursting in front of the bridge, put the navigator out of action and the others burst among the planes, waiting to take off. One after another they began to explode, starting enormous fires. Men staggered, blinded, round the decks, falling over bodies, scorched by flames, suffocating from heat and smoke. Columns of black smoke rose as the carrier lost speed and finally stopped. Within minutes, Yamaguchi's flagship was a helpless hulk, torn apart by the explosions. So great was the apparent damage that the remainder of *Enterprise*'s pilots turned away to bomb one of the Japanese escorting battleships, the *Haruna*.

When what was left of Tomonaga's squadron returned from their attack on *Yorktown* to land on the *Hiryu* she was burning furiously, and they were compelled to circle like fledglings over a burning nest. The fighters attacked the second half of the US strike force – the sixteen Dauntlesses from *Hornet* – which arrived shortly afterward, but shortage of fuel cut short their efforts and one by one all the remaining Japanese planes plunged into the sea. Meanwhile the *Hornet*'s Dauntlesses went on to bomb the battleship *Haruna* and the cruiser *Chikuma*.

For some time it seemed as if the fire in the *Hiryu* might be brought under control, but she was doomed. By midnight she lay helpless on the water, with a list of 15 degrees. Her steering had gone and most of the fire pumps were out of action. Several desperate attempts to fight a way through the smoke and flames to the engine rooms had failed. Like her adversary, *Yorktown*, she was dying.

A brilliant moon provided the backcloth to leaping flames and black smoke when at 0230 hours Admiral Yamaguchi ordered Captain Kaku to summon all hands. Etched against the flames, he addressed the crew from the bridge, 'As officer commanding this carrier division,' he said, 'I am solely responsible for the loss of *Hiryu* and *Soryu*. I shall remain on board to the end. But I command all of you to leave the ship and continue your loyal service to His Majesty the Emperor.' Yamaguchi then took off his black admiral's cap and gave it to his Flag Lieutenant, Commander Ito, as a memento. In return Ito gave him a piece of cloth with which to lash himself to the bridge and make sure he would go down with the ship. Then to the accompaniment of a few desultory *banzais*, *Hiryu*'s flag and the Admiral's were ceremoniously lowered. Some of Yamaguchi's officers asked for permission to die with him, but he ordered them aboard the destroyer *Kazaguma* standing alongside. Only Captain Kaku refused to board the destroyer, insisting that it was his duty as well as his right to stay aboard the blazing carrier with his admiral.

When everyone else had left the ship,

Above: The fires aboard the Japanese carrier *Hiryu* led to her being abandoned.

Right and below right: After second torpedo attack, the listing *Yorktown* was abandoned.

the two men lashed themselves to the helm and waited for her to sink. It seemed that the *Hiryu* was as stubborn about sinking as the *Yorktown*, and at 0510 hours Captain Abe, commander of the escorting destroyer division, gave the order for a *coupe de grâce* to be administered. At 0510 hours two torpedoes found their mark and a couple of deafening explosions followed. The *Hiryu* began to settle down and Abe, satisfied that he had seen the last of the carrier, ordered the destroyers to return. At 0540 hours he reported by radio to Yamamoto that the *Hiryu* had been scuttled. An hour and 20 minutes later, however, a scout plane from the light carrier *Hosho*, which had been sent to locate the Nagumo Force, radioed that the smoldering wreck of the *Hiryu* was still afloat and that men could be seen on board. Yamamoto's reaction was to pass the information to Nagumo, ordering him to verify that the *Hiryu* had gone down and to make every effort to rescue any survivors. Nagumo sent a destroyer and the *Nagara*'s seaplane to do this, but the *Hiryu* was never seen again. It was learned afterward that the *Hiryu* had actually remained afloat until about 0820 hours. The men who had been seen on deck were survivors of the engine-room crew, who had miraculously escaped when Abe's torpedoes blasted an

exit from where they were trapped below decks. Subsequently, after the carrier sank, they were picked up by an American ship and spent the rest of the war in captivity.

About 150 miles away *Yorktown* was also dying. At 1458 hours on 4 June – following Tomonaga's attack – her ebullient commander, Captain Elliot Buckmaster, had given the fateful order 'Abandon ship.' All the available evidence had suggested that *Yorktown* was in danger of sinking, and the decision was undoubtedly correct. Fletcher who had already transferred his flag to the cruiser *Astoria* confirmed the order, and Buckmaster was the last to leave the ship – or so everyone believed at the time. More than 2000 men were taken off the doomed carrier and at 1800 hours the ships that had been standing by moved off to the east. The carrier was now alone, except for the destroyer *Hughes*, which had orders to sink her if she started to burn. (Fire would have given her position away and made possible her capture by the Japanese.) She was still alone, but the list she had taken on earlier seemed to be correcting itself, and Buckmaster, who had never given up hope of saving his vessel, had now concluded that a salvage operation was feasible. That night while he studied ways and means, key men were sought out for a salvage party.

Above: The Japanese submarine *I- 68* sank the damaged *Yorktown.*

Above right: Destroyers stand by the stricken *Yorktown.*

Right: Yorktown survivors parade aboard a rescuing cruiser.

First, it was decided, the flight decks and hangar decks would have to be cleared of debris, in order to lighten the ship. Next, the four 5-inch guns on the port side would have to be cut away. Then, with power furnished by escorting ships, water and oil could be pumped from *Yorktown*'s port tanks to the starboard. This, it was reasoned, would bring the carrier back to an almost even keel. Finally, water tenders would light off the boilers, and *Yorktown* could limp to port on her own power. All this might be speeded up because the fleet tug *Vireo*, moored at French Frigate Shoal, between Midway and Oahu, was already on her way to take *Yorktown* in tow while the work progressed.

With luck all might have gone well, but at 0626 hours on 5 June, the *Hughes* picked up a Japanese scout plane on her radar. It had come from the cruiser *Chikuma* and at 0652 hours its pilot radioed that he had sighted 'an enemy aircraft carrier of the *Yorktown* Class.' This message sealed the *Yorktown*'s fate. As soon as Yamamoto received it he radioed another message to Lieutenant Commander Yahachi Tanabe in the submarine *I-168* off Midway. *I-168* was to 'locate and destroy the American carrier.' Tanabe had just been waiting submerged after bombarding Midway. Now he set a course for *Yorktown*'s estimated position.

A short time later the fleet tug, *Vireo*, arrived and began to make preparations to take *Yorktown* in tow. Sailors from *Hughes*, after making their trip to *Yorktown*, reported that the carrier seemed to be holding her own, and that although the fire had flared up again, it did not seem to pose

serious danger. Almost simultaneously, 20 miles to the east, Captain Buckmaster and his salvage party set off in the destroyer *Hamman*.

By 1200 hours *Yorktown*'s salvage operations were in full swing. The *Vireo* had taken the carrier in tow and was pulling her back toward Hawaii. It was a slow tedious business, and the huge hulk was really more than the little *Vireo* could manage – even at three knots. However, the men working aboard *Yorktown* were making considerable progress, pumping out flooded compartments and cutting away the guns to lighten her. The *Hamman* was then secured along her starboard side, supplying power for the pumps, and five other destroyers circled her to guard against submarine attacks.

Tanabe arrived on the scene at about 1300 hours and the brief action that followed can be counted one of the great submarine exploits of the war. After threading his way under the US destroyer cordon, Tanabe came up to periscope depth. He waited his opportunity, fired four torpedoes, and dived. Aboard the *Yorktown* the salvage party had paused for a lunch of sandwiches and warm Coca-Cola when one of them, standing on the starboard side of the hangar deck, commented, 'Hey, look! There's some black fish.'

Two of the torpedoes hit the *Yorktown*, and when her battered hulk had absorbed the two shocks Buckmaster knew there was no longer any hope for her. *Hamman* had no time to pull clear and one torpedo cut her in two. She sank almost at once, and as she went down her depth charges exploded under water, killing many of the men who

had been thrown overboard or who had dived into the water.

While Buckmaster was again getting his men off his stricken vessels, six US destroyers tried to sink the *I-168*. Tanabe recorded later that he and his men counted 60 near misses by depth charges, and at the end of the attack the *I-168* was crippled – unable to move, with no lights, no pumps working, batteries damaged and chlorine escaping from them. This deadly gas was the submariner's greatest fear. Tanabe watched as a mouse 'staggered drunkenly across my foot.' Then, unexpectedly, the American destroyers broke off the attack. They had been ordered back to *Yorktown* to investigate sonar contacts picked up by two other destroyers. Tanabe, puzzled but relieved, took *I-168* to the surface, using up most of his remaining compressed air. 'When I got to the bridge,' he wrote later, 'there was no sign of the enemy carrier. But between myself and the eastern horizon I could see three American destroyers.' One of them, *Hughes*, saw *I-168* surface and all three destroyers – *Hughes*, *Gwin* and *Monagham* – came about and started pursuit. Tanabe, taking advantage of every second, continued to charge his batteries and refill his air tanks, even as *Hughes* came within range and opened up with her forward 5-inch gun. At the last moment Tanabe submerged, turned 180 degrees, and ran directly under the American destroyers. The trick worked, *I-168* escaped and Tanabe eventually got back to Kure.

Tanabe's victim, *Yorktown*, remained afloat until the following morning (6 June Japanese time, 7 June US time). Then she simply turned over and sank.

6. YAMAMOTO'S REACTION

Not until it was too late did Admiral Yamamoto take any part in the battle which he had wanted to turn into a decisive fleet engagement. At dawn on 4 June his flagship, the *Yamato*, was 800 miles northwest of Midway, and some 300 miles from Nagumo's carriers. Because he had insisted on radio silence it was some hours before the Commander in Chief appreciated the extent of Nagumo's defeat.

At first, everything had seemed to be going well. *Akagi*'s radio silence only seemed to confirm that events were shaping as he had expected. So too did Tomonaga's message reporting the completion of his mission against Midway. To Yamamoto it was quite logical for Tomonaga to suggest a second strike against the atoll as American air strength on Midway had to be eliminated before the Japanese invasion. Surprise, it seemed, had been achieved, and the Commander in Chief and his staff awaited the next message with confidence.

At 0740 hours, the terse flash from the *Tone*'s scout plane saying 'Have sighted 10 ships, apparently enemy,' caused a few speculative frowns. While Yamamoto pondered this message no one spoke. Soon afterward another message from *Tone*'s plane reported, 'American fleet has five cruisers, five destroyers – and one carrier.' Yamamoto glanced at the bridge clock. The timing was perfect. Nagumo's second wave of planes on the deck of the carriers would now be ready to take off and they would soon make short work of the lone American carrier.

Half an hour later, however, came the first indication that all might not be as well as it seemed. From the scout plane came the report, '100 carrier-borne enemy planes heading for the Nagumo Force.' This meant that there must be more than one American carrier, yet Yamamoto still felt confident about the outcome of the forthcoming battle.

For two long hours nothing more was heard from Nagumo's carriers. Then at 1050 hours the chief signals officer, Commander Yoshio Wada, silently handed Admiral Yamamoto a radio message. It was from Rear Admiral Abe in the cruiser *Tone* informing the Commander in Chief of the fate of Nagumo's carriers. Abe's message ran, 'Fires raging aboard *Kaga*, *Soryu* and *Akagi* resulting from attacks by enemy carrier and land-based planes. We plan to

have *Hiryu* engage enemy carriers. We are temporarily withdrawing to the north to assemble our forces.'

The news that three of his carriers were out of action broke Yamamoto's imperturbability. There was only one course open to him now: he must take over the direction of the battle and his battleships must steam toward Midway. This was a decision he should perhaps have taken at the outset of the operation; now it was going to prove too late. No sooner had he decided to steam full ahead to join Nagumo than fog came down. Speed was vital, but it took Yamamoto more than an hour to get his gigantic fleet under way and as it began to steam toward Midway at 20 knots the fog was thickening. The ships followed a zigzag course to avoid the American submarines – a hazardous maneuver in heavy fog, but one which Yamamoto decided he must take if he was to push ahead to help Nagumo.

En route there was an anxious planning conference in the operations cabin of the *Yamato*. While the merits and drawbacks of the proposed operation were being debated Yamamoto said nothing. Then, pale and tight-lipped, he signified that he had decided on a night action.

The destruction of Midway was necessary in order to eliminate it as an American aircraft base. To get things moving, orders were sent to Tanabe in the submarine *I-168* – still patrolling off the atoll – to close in on the island and start shelling the airfield with her 4-inch deck gun. This bombardment was to be kept up until Tanabe was joined by the four heavy cruisers from Kondo's invasion group, *Mikuma*, *Mogami*, *Suzuya* and *Kumano*. The battleship *Hiei* would also join the action as soon as she arrived.

At 1220 hours Yamamoto signalled a general order of the day, 'All forces will attack the enemy in the Midway area.' Half an hour later a more detailed instruction was transmitted, 'Commander (Midway Forces) will dispatch part of his strength to bombard and destroy air bases on Midway. All combat forces from both Midway and Aleutian area will engage the enemy fleet in decisive battle.' Yamamoto was still looking for his one decisive engagement.

How soon Vice-Admiral Kakuda's two carriers *Ryujo* and *Junyo* would reach the battle area was the crucial issue, for if they

arrived in time the Japanese would still have a superiority in carriers. At 1630 hours a signal was received from *Kakuda*. It was not encouraging. Despite dense fog, he had carried out his strike on Dutch Harbor, as planned, but his ships could not be expected to join the Midway battle before the afternoon of 6 June – 48 hours later. Then at 1615 hours Admiral Yamaguchi radioed from *Hiryu*, 'Pilots report enemy force is apparently composed of three carriers, five large cruisers and 15 destroyers. Our attacks succeeded in damaging two carriers.'

At 1736 hours the scout plane from *Chikuma* radioed that the Americans were

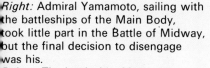

Right: Admiral Yamamoto, sailing with the battleships of the Main Body, took little part in the Battle of Midway, but the final decision to disengage was his.
Below: The battleship *Mutsu*, here firing her broadside, was one of Yamamoto's battleships.

retreating eastward. It was more a hopeful prophecy than a statement of fact. To make it a reality, Yamamoto had ordered his two carriers in the Aleutians, *Ryujo* and *Junyo*, to join him and they were on their way. The carrier *Zuiho*, with the troop convoy, was moving up from the southwest. Within sight of the flagship *Yamato* was the ancient *Hosho*, the world's first carrier built from the keel up. Yamamoto knew he was inferior to the Americans in aircraft strength, even with these reinforcements, but he had overwhelming superiority in total number of ships and guns.

At this point Yamamoto was still determined that the Midway operation should continue. Temporarily, as he saw it, the Japanese had lost control of the air, but the situation was not yet hopeless, and his reinforcements were on their way. Hashimoto's message that *Yorktown* was burning encouraged Yamamoto to cling to the original plan, and so at 1915 hours – an hour and 20 minutes after *Hiryu*'s loss – he sent a message to his command, 'The enemy fleet which has practically been destroyed is retiring. Combined Fleet units in the vicinity are preparing to pursue the remnants and at the same time occupy Midway.' This directive was neither true nor practical with the forces Yamamoto could muster at the moment. The Japanese Commander in Chief must have known this when he dictated the signal, and it must therefore be concluded that it was intended only to boost flagging morale.

As the US fleet withdrew toward the east, hopes of night engagement were failing. Yamamoto persisted. Not only did he want to continue the fight, he also wanted to pick up his burning carriers which yet might be saved. He also had hopes of capturing *Yorktown* – for he knew he could easily deal with the destroyers standing by her – and towing her back to the Inland Sea.

Aboard the *Nagara* there was not the same resolute determination to see the operation through to the bitter end as there was on the *Yamato*. Nagumo's officers had witnessed the destruction of all their carriers and their morale was low. Some were abjectly depressed, but one or two were possessed by a sort of do-or-die hysteria, which centered round a wild plan to throw the destroyers guarding the strike carriers into Yamamoto's night engagement.

Then came a blinker message from *Chikuma*, 'Scout plane sighted five enemy carriers, six cruisers and 15 destroyers 30 miles east of the burning carriers.' The pilot had seen the *Yorktown* adrift, and had then spotted the *Enterprise* and *Hornet*. To evade American fighters he had then been forced to take cover in the clouds and when he came out of them he found the two American carriers a second time. Somehow he must have lost his bearings; everyone by that time was weary and confused. Whatever the reason, he reported finding five carriers. Nagumo, whose heart was no

only 90 miles from Nagumo's fleet – and were withdrawing eastward. Yamamoto had already sent Kondo and his fast battleships racing toward them at top speed. A night action might turn the battle in Japan's favor because the Imperial Navy was better trained for night actions than the Americans. The Americans' superiority in aircraft carriers would not count at night as they were not trained for night-flying operations. The Japanese superiority in numbers might save the day. Sunset was at 1823 hours, and at 1755 hours came the worst news of all, '*Hiryu* hit by bombs and set on fire at 1730 hours': Yamamoto's

last remaining carrier had gone.

Soon after this Yamamoto received Nagumo's message saying that he had left his burning flagship and transferred to the *Nagara*. 'There are still four enemy aircraft carriers,' the signal continued, 'possibly including light aircraft carriers, six cruisers and 16 destroyers. They are steaming westward. None of our aircraft carriers is operational. We plan to contact the enemy with scout aircraft tomorrow morning.' 'Tomorrow morning' was too late for Yamamoto. Earlier he had radioed Tokyo that the American fleet was nearly destroyed and that what was left of it was longer in the battle, was now thoroughly confused. He was certain that his pilots had knocked out two carriers. Yet there was a scout reporting five more – all of them operational.

Meanwhile in Tokyo the Naval General Staff were tensely following the progress of the battle. When the report came in that *Hiryu* had suffered the same fate as *Akagi*, *Kaga* and *Soryu*, they realized the operation was doomed. But did Yamamoto realize it? Like Yamamoto, Admiral Nagano, the Chief of Naval Staff, was not too deeply concerned about Japan's four finest carriers. Even after this disaster, the Imperial Navy still had more warships of every category in the Pacific than the United States. What worried him more was what Admiral Yamamoto, smarting under Nagumo's terrible defeat, might do next. American strength on Midway was not destroyed. Moreover they still had at least one undamaged carrier, if not two. If Yamamoto continued to press home his attack on Midway he might lose the whole Japanese fleet. Yet no orders, no advice, were given by Tokyo. Nagano had decided that it was Admiral Yamamoto's battle and he must fight it as he wished without interference. Nagano simply waited, picking up signals and reading them in silence. It was defeat; he knew it; everyone knew it; no one was willing to be the first to admit it or to call off the operation. That was Yamamoto's decision – and his alone.

At 2130 hours there was a panic-stricken signal from Nagumo, based on the false report of *Chikuma*'s scout plane. 'The total strength of the enemy,' he said, 'is five carriers, six cruisers and 15 destroyers. We are retiring to the northwest escorting *Hiryu* at 15 knots.' Admiral Ugaki, Yamamoto's Chief of Staff, put everyone's thoughts into words when he threw down the second signal and muttered savagely, 'The Nagumo force has no stomach for a night engagement.' Yamamoto silently agreed with him and it was at this point that he decided to relieve Nagumo and put Admiral Kondo in charge of the whole attack force. Kondo, who had shown both good judgment and initiative in the crisis, was already on his way to join the battered remnants of Nagumo's fleet and to attempt to provoke a night battle. With him was a formidable fleet of four fast battleships, nine cruisers and 19 destroyers, all geared for a night surface action.

'Commander in Chief Second Fleet Kondo will take command of Nagumo forces, excepting *Hiryu*, *Akagi* and the ships escorting them,' Yamamoto ordered. This left Nagumo in command of the two blazing half sunken hulks of his remaining carriers, but as far as the battle was concerned, he was relieved from duty.

At midnight the radio transmitter on the flagship *Yamato* was still busily signalling orders to Kakuda to rendezvous as soon as possible with remnants of Nagumo's fleet. It was also ordering Kondo to prepare for a decisive surface action. Yet even as the signal went out it was becoming increasingly evident that there was little hope of contacting the American fleet before dawn.

In spite of their victory against the Japanese carriers it was a nervous night for both American admirals as they tried to assess the results of the day's battle. Fletcher's task force, maimed by the loss of *Yorktown*, sheltered behind *Hornet* and *Enterprise*. Although the Japanese carriers had gone, Spruance still feared the appearance of Yamamoto's big battleships. He was fully aware that Yamamoto might yet restore the balance by bringing them in for a surface engagement. Now that he was in tactical command of the Pacific fleet, he was determined not to fall into a trap, and so he decided to sail east during the night. Later he said, 'I did not feel justified in risking a night encounter with possibly superior enemy forces. Nor did I wish to be too far from Midway next morning. I wanted to be in a position from which to either follow up the retreating enemy or break up a landing attack on Midway.'

Admiral Spruance did not believe it was likely that the Japanese would try to land on Midway after losing their four carriers, but it was a possibility which could not be disregarded, and Midway had to be protected. Having pulled back to a position which would allow him sea room to maneuver if Yamamoto decided to commit his battleships, he kept his task force in the same approximate area about 250 miles northwest of the atoll.

On Midway itself Tomonaga's mission and a series of confusing messages and radio intercepts had made it a trying and anxious day. Tomonaga's attack was seen at first as the foretaste of disaster, and seven of the atoll's Flying Fortresses were ordered back to Oahu. There, it was presumed, they would be needed in the battle for Hawaii, which would surely follow the fall of Midway. Midway's air strength was now down to two fighters, 12 dive bombers, 18 Catalinas and four serviceable Fortresses.

Above: B-17 defensive armament had to be increased after combat experience.
Left: A Dauntless with its fuel exhausted ditches alongside a cruiser.

Below: Despite its high performance, the Zero failed to protect the Japanese carriers at Midway.

In the afternoon Midway learned of the crippling of the four Japanese carriers and the four Fortresses were sent on a strike against Nagumo's battered fleet. Their pilots returned claiming that their bombs had struck some of the Japanese ships. They also returned with some alarming news: they had been attacked by Zeros on their mission. If four carriers had indeed been sunk, the fact that Zeros were still flying suggested that there was a fifth somewhere around. The possibility that the Japanese fighters were from the doomed *Hiryu*, using up their last drop of fuel before ditching, was never considered.

At dusk 11 American Marine dive bombers took off to find the fifth carrier, but heavy squalls and a moonless sky defeated their search. Getting back to base was also a problem. Only the blue blur from their exhausts kept them together and only the fires on Midway started by Tomonaga's raid guided them home.

Both the Midway Command and Spruance were alarmed by the possibility of a fifth carrier in the vicinity, and tension which had begun to relax rapidly built up again. Unconfirmed alarmist reports at once

Above: Midway saw the operational debut of the Grumman TBF Avenger.

began to circulate. At 2100 hours one of the patrol boats reported a landing on the small island of Kure, 60 miles to the west. This suggested that the invasion was imminent. Back at Pearl Harbor, the Pacific Fleet submarine commander, Rear Admiral Robert English also believed this and pulled his boats back to a five-mile radius round Midway. At midnight two Catalinas took off armed with torpedoes in readiness to attack the approaching ships while the garrison prepared itself. Eighty-five 500-pound bombs were loaded by hand and 45,000 gallons of gasoline were hand pumped into the planes.

The tension reached its climax at around 0100 hours, when Tanabe's submarine – acting in accordance with the orders he had received from Yamamoto's alert at 2030 hours – surfaced in the lagoon, and a shell winged its way toward Midway. Five more followed in quick succession before two searchlights pinpointed the submarine. Shore batteries began firing back and their aim was effective. Shells bracketed *I-168* almost at once and the disappointed Tanabe had no choice but to beat a hasty retreat. He headed south, away from the island, shaking off surface pursuers. Angry and disappointed, Tanabe assumed that *I-168* has finished its job for this battle. (He had not yet been told to find and sink the crippled *Yorktown*.)

On Midway the garrison was waiting for the attack which they believed to be imminent. Two hundred miles away Spruance also thought that the shelling was the prelude to invasion, and his view was confirmed when the US submarine *Tambor* reported 'many unidentified ships' only 90 miles from Midway. There were the heavy cruisers *Mogami* and *Mikuma* and their escorts – part of the vanguard of the occupation force, now on their way under Yamamoto's orders to relieve the *I-168* and shell the atoll. Spruance thought this might be a landing force and he gave orders for his fleet to steam toward Midway at 25 knots.

Spruance began sailing toward the atoll at full speed, Yamamoto was sitting in his operations room on his flagship reassessing the situation. He now knew that the Americans had at least two carriers still operational and that by sailing east they had managed to dodge a night action. Yamamoto had also received more depressing news. His fleet was sailing 19 degrees off course. This meant all hope of a night battle was lost. *Yorktown*, too, was obviously sinking, so he gave up the idea of capturing her. If he continued on his present course his own ships would almost certainly be attacked by planes at dawn.

A madcap attempt to snatch victory from disaster was now proposed by the Chief Operations Officer, Rear Admiral Kuroshima. The *Yamato*, he suggested, should lead the battleship flotilla to Midway in broad daylight and shell the shore installations. The invasion would then go on. Rear Admiral Ugaki, the officer who had 'bent' the Midway war games in favor of the assault, was appalled. 'Engaging shore installations with only surface craft is stupid,' he said. 'A large number of American planes are still based on Midway. Some of the enemy carriers are still intact. Our battleships will be destroyed by enemy air and submarine attacks before we could even get close enough to use our big guns.'

Ugaki had, perhaps, indulged in fantasies during the war games, but basically he was a sane and level-headed man, prepared to take a realistic point of view. The Imperial Navy, he argued, must accept that it has been defeated at Midway. This did not mean that Japan had lost the war. Nor was the sinking of the four carriers so much of a calamity; including those nearly completed, the Navy still had eight carriers. However if Yamamoto acted rashly now a minor setback could turn into a catastrophic defeat. 'In battle,' he added, 'as in chess, it is a fool who lets himself be led into a reckless move through desperation.'

Ugaki's intervention scotched Kuroshima's scheme. Not all Yamamoto's staff officers were satisfied. To some, the need to 'save face' was paramount and they were prepared to gamble everything for a chance to do so. Eventually one individual voiced his worries. 'How can we apologize to His Majesty for this defeat?' he asked.

Yamamoto had not spoken during the discussion, but his sternly set features broke as he replied abruptly, 'Leave that to me, I am the only one who must apologize to His Majesty.' From this brief comment it is evident that Yamamoto – the shrewd, aggressive cardplayer – had all but decided to abandon the Midway operation.

7. RETREAT

t was after midnight on 5 June when amamoto figuratively folded his hands and ancelled Operation Midway. Admiral Kondo's fleet, still racing toward a night ttack on the US carriers and the bombard- nent of the atoll, was ordered to withdraw nd join him at a rendezvous where all the hips would refuel for the long voyage ome. Some two and a half hours later

Below: Mikuma sank at Midway.

(at 0255 hours on 6 June) he ordered Ichiki's troopships to make their way back to Japan. The operation was definitely over, all that remained now was the humiliating and hazardous task of rounding up the scattered elements of the Combined Fleet and getting them out of the battle area without being discovered by US scout planes or submarines.

When the four heavy cruisers assigned by Kondo to the task of shelling Midway

received a message to say the operation was cancelled, they turned about. This was the force of unidentified ships picked up earlier by the US submarine *Tambor*, and when the Japanese ships changed course, the *Tambor* followed. In the race eastward toward Midway, the Japanese cruisers had been unable to keep pace with the destroyers so that when the order cancelling their mission was received they were unprotected. Suddenly a lookout on Vice-Admiral Takeo

Right: The Japanese destroyer *Yukikaze* escorted the Transport Group of the Midway Occupation Force. Her main armament comprised 5-inch guns and torpedo tubes firing the famous 'long lance.'
Below: A US Navy gun crew member updates his scoreboard.

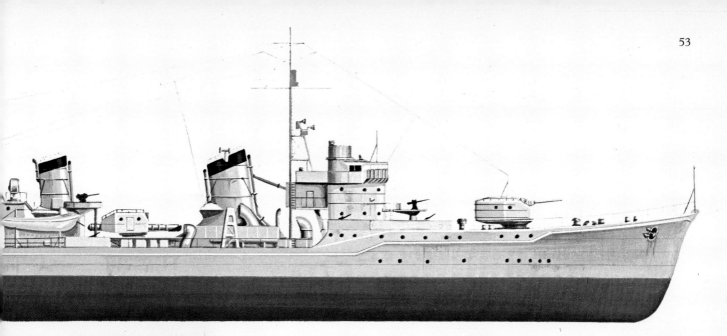

Left: The Dauntless dive bomber emerged from the Battle of Midway with an enviable reputation as a warplane. It was to remain in front-line service until 1944.
Right: The US Marine Corps defenders of Midway produced this suitably bellicose view of the battle.
Below: Four heavy cruisers of the *Takao* Class, *Takao, Maya, Atago* and *Chokai,* served in the Midway operation. Their main armament was 10 8-inch guns.

Above: Vought SB2U Vindicators of the 2nd Marine Air Wing were based on Midway Island.

Left: Mikuma was sunk by Dauntlesses from USS *Enterprise* on 6 June.

Kurita's flagship, *Kumano*, spotted the *Tambor* which had just surfaced for better observation. Panic ensued as the *Kumaro* flashed orders for an immediate 45 degree turn to port. The signal, 'Red! Red!' was blinked to the *Suzuya* next astern and the *Kumaro* swung left. *Suzuya*, in turn, relayed the signal and also turned left, as did the third ship *Mikuma*. It was two hours before sunrise, and it was dark and foggy. Tension had relaxed when the cruisers turned away from Midway and this may account for the lack of vigilance. Whatever the cause, *Mogami*, the last ship in line, failed to get the emergency turn signal in time and collided with *Mikuma*. Although the cruisers had reduced their speed since they had turned about, they were still making about 28 knots and consequently the *Mogami*'s bow was damaged and one of *Mikuma*'s oil tanks was holed.

When he was told of the accident, Admiral Kurita turned back to see what help he could give. When *Mogami*'s skipper, Captain Akira Soyi, reported that he could make 12 knots, Kurita decided to push on to the rendezvous, leaving the *Mikuma* and two destroyers, the *Arashio* and the *Asashio*, as escort for the *Mogami*. Dawn was breaking by this time and men in the four ships were gazing apprehensively at the sky in anticipation of an attack by American aircraft. They did not have long to wait.

Morale in Yamamoto's fleet was now at a low ebb. During the night some of Nagumo's destroyers had ferried casualties from the four carriers to Yamamoto's battleships where better medical facilities were available. The sea was rough, making it impossible for the destroyers to get alongside the battleships, so the transferring the wounded was a slow process. All through the pitch-dark night the casualties were pulled aboard by ropes attached to bamboo stretchers. By dawn the sick bays and crew quarters of the four battleships were jammed with wounded, most of them burn victims. Witnessing this scene, every sailor in the battleships became aware that the Imperial Navy had just suffered a great and crushing defeat. Few could console themselves for the loss of the four great carriers by the fact that their main battleship

strength remained intact. After what had happened to them, they knew better than anyone that big guns were as useless as bows and arrows in the Pacific.

Throughout the hours of darkness Yamamoto's battleships headed east to link up with Nagumo and Kondo withdrawing west. The sun rose at 0440 hours and the sky was clear and cloudless. Visibility was about 40 miles and as the morning progressed it seemed that this was the best weather they had had since the Japanese had left home waters. It was ideal weather for aircraft, and sentries stared warily at the open sky, watching for signs of US planes.

Kondo's main force linked up with Yamamoto at about 0700 hours, when both fleets were then 320 miles northwest of Midway. Five hours later Nagumo's battered ships appeared on the horizon. Standing on the bridge under the hot Pacific sun, Yamamoto silently watched them approach. The returning ships bore little resemblance to the proud fleet that had sailed so confidently out of the Inland Sea only 10 days before. The carriers were gone and many of the destroyers were missing; some of them were still picking up survivors of the battle clinging to oil-slippery wreckage.

By dawn on 6 June Spruance had realized that the Japanese were pulling back. Between then and 0800 hours Midway planes reported that all Japanese vessels within their range were withdrawing, and he was now convinced that Yamamoto was retreating. The submarine *Tambor*, which was still doggedly trailing the twin cruisers, now identified them as *Mogami* and *Mikuma*, steaming fast 175 miles away. There were several other ships over 250 miles away, but there was no sign of Nagumo's carriers. The only evidence that they had ever existed was the shape of the oil patches on the water.

Now that the Japanese were leaving the battle area Spruance sent every available plane to harry and destroy them. The 12 Marine bombers left on Midway – six Vindicators led by Captain Richard Fleming and six Dauntlesses led by Captain Marshall Tyler – took off to follow *Mikuma*'s clearly visible oil trail. At 0805 hours

Mikuma's captain reported 'waves of dive bombers,' as the Dauntlesses dived on her sister ship the *Mogami*. Then the Vindicators swooped down on *Mikuma*. Fleming's engine was hit by a shell but he held his course and dropped his bomb. Pilots coming behind him watched his plane smash into *Mikuma's* after turret.

Meanwhile Spruance's carriers were steaming up to close the gap, and it was not long before planes from the *Enterprise* discovered the *Mogami* and the *Mikuma*, limping along 150 miles away. Three successive attacks were made and repeated hits were scored on the two damaged cruisers. Although her captain tried hard to head for the nearest Japanese base at Wake Island, the *Mikuma* was sinking fast.

Above: The Aichi D3A 'Val' dive bombers suffered heavily at Midway and thereafter gradually disappeared from front-line units.
Top: The Grumman F4F-4 Wildcat was the standard fighter in the US Navy in 1942–43 and was credited with over 900 victories in air combat.

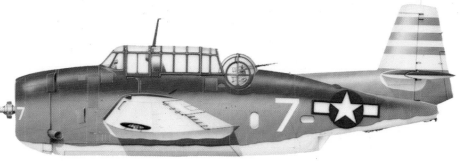

Above: Five of the six Grumman TBF Avengers participating in Midway were lost, but the type went on to become one of the classic warplanes of World War II.
Top: A Douglas SBD Dauntless of US Marine Squadron VMB-1.
Below: After its early successes in the Pacific War, the Mitsubishi A6M 'Zero' performed less well from Midway onward as Allied fighter pilots learned to exploit the aircraft's inherent weaknesses.

At 1200 hours, as the third attack force flew away, she suddenly turned over and went down – taking 1000 men with her. Apart from carriers, the *Mikuma* was the largest Japanese surface warship to be sunk since the beginning of the war. She had always fought with her sister ship *Mogami*, and she perished in *Mogami*'s defense when she deliberately drew down bombers upon herself.

The *Mogami*, also fighting fiercely to protect herself and her sister ship, received heavy bomb damage and lost her bow, but although listing heavily she was still able to steam along at 20 knots. She was the last Japanese warship to get clear of the American planes in the Midway battle. Escorted by destroyers she managed to creep back to Truk, but she was out of the war for more than a year.

Next on Spruance's list was the burning Japanese carrier *Hiryu* which he thought was still afloat. In fact she had sunk hours before. In the early afternoon 12 B-17s took off from Midway to locate her. All they found was the destroyer *Tanikaze* which Nagumo had sent to rescue survivors from *Hiryu* if she were still afloat. *Tanikaze* was steaming back to report *Hiryu*'s fate when the Fortresses swooped on her. They made two attacks, dropping 80 bombs, but the fast-moving destroyer was too quick for them and they achieved only a few near-misses.

The two American carriers *Hornet* and *Enterprise* were now about 130 miles from Midway and the gap between them and the fleeing Japanese was widening. So that they could carry maximum fuel, Spruance ordered the bombers to take off armed only with a single 500-pound bomb each. In his anxiety to achieve the biggest kill possible, he held the attack back until 1500 hours while his two carriers steamed at full speed to close the range. This late takeoff meant that his planes could not return before dark and the carriers would have to light up their flight decks to recover them. Spruance, who still believed he was pursuing the fourth Japanese carrier, *Hiryu*, accepted the risk. Again his planes found only the much-harried *Tanikaze* and they attacked her with no more success than the B-17s. Darkness descended as

they flew back and *Enterprise* and *Hornet* switched on deck and searchlights to guide them in. This was a risk because the lights made them a sitting target for any Japanese submarine lurking in the area. Spruance was more concerned about his pilots, as most of them had never before landed on a carrier at night. They all came in safely on the illuminated deck, except one who landed in the sea and was rescued later.

Now that it was dark and the American carriers were approaching the bad weather area, Spruance decided to call it a day. His fuel was running low and his pilots were exhausted from two days of almost continuous operations. He had been informed that there were no Japanese warships for more than 250 miles ahead, but he was not

Above: Shokaku missed the Midway battle but was sunk in the Philippine Sea in June 1944.

Left: Dauntlesses of Scouting Squadron 64 over the Solomons in April 1943.

going to risk running into any of Yamamoto's big battleships in the dark where they would pound him to pieces. In addition he was approaching the 700-mile flying range of Wake Island, where he believed the Japanese had flown a large number of planes in readiness for a landing on Midway after its capture. So Spruance changed course west to rendezvous with a tanker Admiral Nimitz had sent out for his ships.

It was a wise decision for Yamamoto was again spoiling for a fight. His ships were over 600 miles from Midway on the day they were to have invaded it, and he was still looking for an opportunity to convert defeat into victory. The attacks on *Tanikaze, Mogami* and *Mikuma* had given him a plain indication that the American carriers were not far away, and he correctly judged that if he turned south he would meet them. At 1200 hours on 6 June he ordered seven cruisers and eight destroyers to make their way toward the crippled *Mogami*. Surrounded by his other battleships, he ordered the *Yamato* to head in the same direction.

At this juncture Yamamoto believed that he was opposed by one carrier, two other ships which had been converted to carriers, and several cruisers and destroyers. If this fleet were lured on westward by the stricken *Mogami* an opportunity might yet occur for the Japanese to strike a decisive blow. With any luck, Kondo's cruisers would be able to engage the Americans during the night, or Yamamoto's

battleships take them the following morning. Control of the air was vital if the battle was to turn in Yamamoto's favor, but as the Japanese could muster a total of about 100 planes – including those of the carriers *Hosho* and *Zuiho* and the seaplanes of the battleships, cruisers and tenders – this was just feasible. To make it certain, however, it was desirable to lure the American fleet to within range of the 50 medium bombers based on Wake Island. (These planes could already reach to within a few miles of where the *Mikuma* had sunk.)

Had Spruance not changed course that evening and called off the chase the Americans would have fallen into Yamamoto's trap. It was not to be. A combination of factors – the need to refuel and refit his carriers, the tiredness of his crews, bad weather and above all a canny suspicion that caution was needed caused Spruance to turn back. Yamamoto pursued his grandiose scheme until the morning of 7 June. Then, with no enemy in sight and his ships in need of fuel, the plan was finally abandoned and he turned for home.

Further attempts were made by the Americans to hit the retreating Japanese fleet by the Midway-bound Fortresses. No contacts were made and when the pilots of the Fortresses returned to Midway the greatest sea battle since Trafalgar was over. It had lasted 48 hours and had been won in the five minutes when American dive bombers caught Nagumo's carriers with their flight decks lined with planes.

APPENDIX

US and Japanese Losses in the Battle of Midway

US losses

Japanese claims about the losses and damage inflicted at the Battle of Midway were grossly exaggerated. Actual losses, quoted in American sources, are given. The unamended Japanese figures are also included for comparison.

Actual losses			Japanese claims		
Ships			Ships		
Sunk: carrier *Yorktown*, destroyer *Hammann*			Sunk: 2 *Enterprise* Class carriers		
			1 *San Francisco* Class heavy cruiser		
			1 destroyer		
Aircraft			Aircraft		
Shot down or destroyed in Midway air strike		45	US carrier-borne aircraft lost		109
US carriers		15	US shore-based aircraft lost		
Shot down by combat air patrol		90	Marine	28	
Shot down by antiaircraft fire of Japanese ships		29	Navy	6	
			Army	4	
	Total	179	Total shore based		38
				Total	147

Damage to ground installations
Eastern Island
1 hangar damaged by fire, 3 buildings damaged by fire, airstrip damaged

Sand Island
1 seaplane hangar damaged by fire, seaplane platform destroyed, 2 fuel storage tanks damaged by fire, 2 anti-aircraft emplacements destroyed

Damage to ground installations
Eastern Island
Marine command post and mess hall destroyed, powerhouse damaged, airstrip damaged but still usable
Sand Island
Seaplane hangar destroyed, fuel storage tanks destroyed, aviation fueling system damaged, hospital and storehouses set on fire

Japanese Losses
Ships
Sunk: 4 carriers (*Akagi, Kaga, Hiryu, Soryu*), 1 heavy cruiser (*Mikuma*)
Severely damaged: 1 heavy cruiser (*Mogami*)
Moderately damaged: 2 destroyers (*Arashio, Asashio*)
Slightly damaged: 1 battleship (*Haruna*), 1 destroyer (*Tanikaze*) 1 tanker (oiler)
(*Akebono Maru*)
Aircraft
Lost in Midway air strike   6
Fighters of combat air patrol
failed to return   12
Lost in attacks on US carriers   24
Lost with carriers when they sank   280   (approximate)
Seaplanes lost   10   (approximate)
                    Total   332*

*US sources quote a figure of approximately 250 planes lost, and this figure of 332, taken from Japanese sources, exceeds the actual operational complement of Nagumo's four carriers (262 planes). The difference partially accounted for by the fact that the Japanese losses include fighter aircraft of the Midway Expeditionary Forces which was being ferried to Midway in these carriers.

Summary of Opposing Forces in the Battle of Midway

The Composition of the Japanese Task Force for 'Operation MI' against Midway

The task force proper was composed of five major tactical groups, some of them subdivided into two or more subgroups. There was also a land-based air force group which is shown as group 6.
Overall command was vested in Admiral Yamamoto aboard the *Yamato*; Rear Admiral Matome Ugaki, his Chief of Staff, travelled with him. All groups moved to the operational area independently.

1. The Advance Expeditionary Force

Vice-Admiral Teruhisa Konatsu in the light cruiser *Katori* (flagship of the sixth Fleet) at Kwajalein

Submarine Squadron 3
Rear Admiral Chimaki Kono, submarines *I-168, I-171, I-175* deployed between latitude 20°N, longitude 166°20′W, and latitude 23°30′N, and longitude 166°20′W.

Submarine Squadron 5
Rear Admiral Tadashige Daigo, submarines *I-156, I-157, I-158, I-159, I-162, I-164, I-165, I-166*, deployed between latitude 28°20′N, longitude 162°20′W, and latitude 26°N, longitude 165°W.

Submarine Squadron 13
Captain Takeharu Miyazaki, submarines *I-121, I-122, I-123* for transporting fuel and oil to French Frigate Shoals and other islands en route to Pearl Harbor.

Below: USS *Yorktown* during the first attack at the Battle of Midway.

2. The First Carrier Striking Force: Vice-Admiral Chuichi Nagumo
Carrier Division 1
Admiral Nagumo carriers *Akagi* (flagship), *Kaga*; 42 fighters, 42 dive bombers, 51 torpedo bombers

Carrier Division 2
Rear Admiral Tamon Yamaguchi, carriers *Hiryu* (flagship), *Soryu*; 42 fighters, 42 dive bombers, 42 torpedo bombers

Support Group
Rear Admiral Hiroaki Abe, battleships *Haruna*, *Kirishima*; heavy cruisers *Tone* (flagship), *Chikuma*

Screening Group
Rear Admiral Susumu Kimura, light cruiser *Nagara* (flagship); destroyers, *Kazagumo*, *Yugumo*, *Makigumo*, *Akigumo*, *Isokaze*, *Urakaze*, *Hamakaze*, *Tanikaze*, *Arashi*, *Nowaki*, *Hagikaze*, *Maikaze*; supply ships *Kyokuto Maru*, *Shinkoku Maru*, *Toho Maru*, *Nippon Maru*, *Kokuyo Maru*

3. Midway Occupation Force: Vice-Admiral Nobutake Kondo

Covering Group
Admiral Kondo, battleships *Kongo*, *Hiei*; heavy cruisers *Atago* (flagship) *Chokai*, *Myoku*, *Haguro*; light cruiser *Yara*; light carrier *Zuiho* (12 fighters, 12 torpedo bombers); destroyers *Murasame*, *Harusame*, *Yudachi*, *Samidare*, *Asagumo*, *Miegumo*, *Natsugumo*, *Miyazuki*; supply ships *Genyo Maru*, *Kenyo Maru*, *Sata*, *Tsurumi*; repair ship *Akami*

Support Group
Rear Admiral Takeo Kurita, heavy cruisers *Kumano* (flagship), *Suzuya*, *Mikuma*, *Mogami*; destroyers *Asashio*, *Arashio*; supply ship *Nichiei Maru*

Transport Group
Rear Admiral Raizo Tanaka, light cruiser *Jintsu* (flagship); 12 transports and freighters carrying 'Kure' and 'Yokosuka,' 5th Special Naval Landing Forces and Army Ichiki Detachment; two construction battalions 'Survey Group,' weather group, etc (about 5000 officers and men); oiler *Akebono Maru*; patrol boats 1, 2, 3, 4, carrying assault detachments; SNLF; destroyers *Kuroshio*, *Oyashio*, *Hatsukaze*, *Yukikaze*, *Amatsukaze*, *Tokitsukaze*, *Kasumi*, *Arare*, *Kagero*, *Shiranuhi*

Seaplane Tender Group
Rear Admiral Ruitero Fujita, seaplane carriers *Chitose* (16 seaplanes [floats], 4 scout planes), *Kamikawa Maru* (8 seaplanes, 2 scout planes), these 30 planes were to be established at a base on Kure Island; destroyer *Hayashio*, patrol boat No 35

4. The Main Body (First Fleet)
Admiral Yamamoto, battleships *Yamato* (Combined Fleet flagship); *Nagato*, *Mutsu*; light carrier *Hosho* (8 Type-96 bombers); light cruiser *Sendai*; destroyers *Fubuki*, *Shirayuki*, *Hatsuyuki*, *Murakumo*, *Isonami*, *Uranami*, *Shikinami*, *Ayanami*, *Amagiri*, *Asagiri*, *Yugiri*, *Shirakumo*; seaplane carriers *Chiyoda*, *Nigshin* (carrying 2 motor torpedo boats and 6 midget submarines

Aleutian Support Force Department
Vice-Admiral Shiro Takasu, battleships *Hyugu* (flagship), *Ise*, *Fuso*, *Yamashiro*; light cruisers *Oi*, *Kikama*; supply ships *Toli Maru*, *Naruto*, *San Clemte Maru*, *Toa Maru*

5. The Northern (Aleutians) Force: Vice-Admiral Moshiro Hosogaya
Main Body of Northern Force
Heavy cruiser *Nachi* (flagship), 2 destroyers

Second Carrier Striking Force
Rear Admiral Kakuji Kakuta, light carrier *Ryujo* (flagship, 16 fighters, 21 torpedo bombers); carrier *Junyo* (24 fighters, 21 dive bombers); heavy cruisers *Maya*, *Takao*; 3 destroyers.

Attu Invasion Force
Rear Admiral Sentaro Omori, light cruiser *Abukuma* (flagship); 4 destroyers; 1 minelayer; 1 transport carrying Army Landing Force (1200 troops)

6. Land-based Air Force: Vice-Admiral Nishizo Tsukahara
Midway Expeditionary Force
Captain Chisato Morita, 36 fighters (transported by carriers); 10 land bombers (at Wake);
6 flying boats (at Jaluit)

24th Air Flotilla
Rear Admiral Minoru Maeda

Chitose Air Group
Captain Fujiro Ohashi, 26 fighters; 36 torpedo bombers (at Kwajalein and Wake)

1st Air Group
Captain Samaji Inouye, 36 fighters; 36 torpedo bombers (at Aur and Wotje)

14th Air Group
18 flying boats (at Jaluit and Wotje)

Commander in Chief, Admiral Chester W Nimitz

Deployment and Composition of the United States Pacific Fleet during the Coral Sea and Midway battles

1. Carrier Striking Force: Rear Admiral Frank J Fletcher

Task Force 17: Admiral Fletcher
carrier *Yorktown* (25 fighters, 19 scout planes, 18 bombers, 13 torpedo bombers);
cruisers *Astoria, Portland*; destroyers *Hammann, Hughes, Morris, Anderson, Russell, Gwin*

Task Force 16: Rear Admiral Raymond A Spruance
carriers *Enterprise* (27 fighters, 19 scout planes, 19 bombers, 14 torpedo bombers),
Hornet (27 fighters, 18 scout planes, 19 bombers, 15 torpedo bombers); cruisers
New Orleans, Minneapolis, Vincennes, Northampton, Pensacola, Atlanta; destroyers
Phelps, Worden, Monaghan, Aylwin, Balch, Coryngham, Benham, Ellet, Maury: supply
ships (oilers) *Cimarron, Platte, Dewey, Monssen*

2. Submarines: under operational control of Rear Admiral Robert H English at Pearl
Harbor

Midway Patrol Group
*Cachalot, Flying Fish, Tambour, Trout, Grayling, Nautilus, Grouper, Dolphin, Gato,
Cuttlefish, Gudgeon, Grenadier*

'Roving Short-Stop' Group
Narwhal, Plunger, Trigger

North of Oahu Patrol
Tarpon, Pike, Finback, Growler.

3. Land-based aircraft, Midway 4 June 1942 – Captain Cyril T Simard
  32 Catalina seaplanes and 6 torpedo bombers from 1 and 2 US Northern Patrol
  27 fighters and 27 dive bombers for the Marine Aircraft Group 22 (2nd Marine Air
  Wing)
  4 B-26 and 19 B-17 bombers of Seventh Army Air Force

4. Local Defenses Midway – Captain Simard
5th Marine Defense Battalion, 8PT (Motor Torpedo) Boats and 4 small patrol craft
The following were also deployed among the islands in the Hawaiian Group:
tenders *Thornton, Ballard*, French Frigate Shoals, destroyer *Clark*, French Frigate
Shoals, oiler *Kaloli*, Pearl and Hermes Reef, Cvt yacht *Crystal*, Pearl and Hermes Reef,
sweeper *Vireo*, Pearl and Hermes Reef. 4 Patrol Vessels.
There was also a Midway Relief Fuelling Unit (which left Pearl Harbor on 3 June and
arrived at Midway three days later) comprising the following:
oiler *Guadaloupe*; destroyers *Blue* and *Ralph Talbot.*

INDEX

Abe, Captain: 42
Abe, Chief Petty Officer: 36
Abe, Rear Admiral: 46
Akagi: 14, 17, 21, 22, 23, 26, 27, 28, 39,
  30, 32–35, 37, 41, 46, 48
Akebono Maru: 25
Amagai, Commander T: 35, 36
Aoki, Captain: 30, 34, 35
Arashio: 55
Asashio: 55
Astoria: 42
Attu: 17
Avenger: 28

British Far Eastern Fleet: 6
Brockman, Lieutenant Commander W: 35
Buckmaster, Captain E: 42, 44
Buffalo: 27

Ceylon: 6, 7, 9, 17
Chikuma: 22, 26, 42, 44, 46, 47, 48

D-Day: 17
  +1: 17
Devastator torpedo bomber: 30, 31, 32
Doolittle, Colonel: 13, 17
Dutch Harbor: 17, 20, 25, 46

Eastern Island: 17
English, Rear Admiral R: 50
Enterprise: 13, 17, 18, 20, 26, 27, 30, 32,
  39, 41, 42, 47, 48, 56, 58–59

Fleming, Captain R: 55–56
Fletcher, Rear Admiral: 20, 25, 26, 27,
  30, 31, 37, 41, 42, 48
French Frigate Shoal: 23, 44
Fuso: 20, 23

Gay, Ensign G: 32
Guam: 21, 23
Gwin: 44

Hagikaze: 35
Halsey, Vice-Admiral W F: 13, 20
Hamaka: 36
Hammann: 44
Haruna: 14, 22, 26, 42
Hashimoto: 40, 47
Hashirajima Anchorage: 17, 21
Hawaii: 6, 13, 15, 23, 44, 48
Hermes: 7
Hiei: 46
Hiroaki, Rear Admiral: 22
Hiroshima Bay: 17, 20
Hiryu: 14, 22, 27, 29, 30, 32, 37, 39–40,
  41, 42, 46, 47, 48, 49, 58
Hornet: 13, 17, 18, 20, 26, 30, 32, 39, 41,
  42, 47, 48, 58–59
Hosho: 15, 23, 42, 47, 59
Hosko: 15
Hosogaya, Vice-Admiral M: 15, 21, 22
Hughes: 42, 44
Hyugu: 20, 23

I-168, submarine: 27, 44, 46, 50
Ichiki, Colonel K: 21, 23, 25, 26, 51

Ise: 20, 23
Isokaze: 36
Ito, Commander: 42
Iwakuni: 17

Japan: 6, 22
Japanese army: 6, 14
  High Command: 6
  Attu Invasion Force: 23
  Carrier Strike Force: 14, 21, 22, 23, 26
  Carrier Task Force: 22, 25
  Combined Fleet: 6, 14, 17, 22, 47, 48, 50
  First Air Fleet: 7
  General Staff: 13
  High Command: 6
  Intelligence: 17, 20, 23, 26
  Kiska Invasion Force: 22, 29
  'Main Body': 14, 15, 17, 21, 25
  Midway Occupation Force: 14-15, 17, 46
  Navy Day: 21
  Northern Area Force: 14, 15, 17, 21, 22
  Second Fleet: 7, 21, 23, 48
  Submarine Advance Expeditionary Force: 14-15, 17, 18
  Support Force: 21, 23
  Supreme Command: 6
Jiutsu: 23
Junyo: 15, 17, 21, 25, 46, 47

Kaga: 14, 22, 26, 27, 28, 30, 32, 34, 35-36, 41, 46, 48
Kaku, Captain T: 41, 42
Kakuda, Rear-Admiral K: 15, 17, 46, 48
Kate: 27
Kawanishi flying boat: 23
Kazaguma: 42
Kimigayu: 36
Kimmel, Admiral: 6
Kimura, Rear Admiral S, 22
Kirishima: 14, 22
Kobayashi, Lieutenant M: 37-39
Konda, Admiral N: 15, 21, 48, 50, 59
  Vice-Admiral: 7, 17, 23, 25, 47, 55
Kumano: 46, 55
Kunisada, Lieutenant Commander Y: 35
Kure Island: 21, 22, 44, 50
Kurita, Rear Admiral T: 21, 23, 50. 51-55
Kuroshima, Rear Admiral: 50
Kusaka, Rear Admiral: 17, 34, 35

Lexington: 13, 18, 23

Makigumo: 36
Maikaze: 35
McClusky, Lieutenant Commander C: 32, 34, 35
Midway Island: 17
  air base: 46
Mikuma: 46, 50, 55-58, 59
Mitscher, Captain M: 13
Miura, Commander: 35
Mogami: 46, 50, 55-56, 58, 59
Monaghan: 44
Musashi: 15
Mutsu: 20, 23

Nagano, Admiral O: 6, 14, 48
Nagara: 22, 37, 42, 47
Nagato: 20, 23

Nagumo, Vice-Admiral: 7, 9, 17, 18, 21-22, 23, 25, 26, 27, 38, 29, 30, 32, 34-35, 37, 42, 46, 47-48, 49, 55, 58, 59
Nautilus: 35
Necker Island: 23
New Guinea: 9, 13
Nimitz, Admiral C W: 6, 17-18, 20, 22, 23, 25, 26, 59
Nishibayashi, Lieutenant Commander: 35

Oahu: 15, 17, 23, 44, 48
Ogawa, Lieutenant S: 27
Okada, Captain J: 23
Ominato: 23
Operation MI: 6-7, 13, 14, 17

Rat Island: 25
Reid, Ensign J: 25
Roosevelt, T: 13
Ryujo: 15, 17, 21, 25, 46, 47

Sand Island: 17, 27-28
Saratoga: 17, 18
Settsu: 17
Shannon, Lieutenant Colonel H: 17, 18
Shoho: 13
Shokaku: 13, 17
Simard, Commander C: 17, 18
Soryu: 14, 22, 27, 29, 30, 32, 34, 36, 37, 39, 41, 42, 46, 48
Soyi, Captain A: 55
Spruance, Rear Admiral R: 20, 27, 30, 31, 32, 48, 49, 50, 55-56, 58, 59
Suganomai, Lieutenant M: 27
Suzuya: 46, 55

Takagi, Vice-Admiral: 21
Takasu, Vice-Admiral: 17
Tambor: 50, 51, 55
Tampo, Commander: 35
Tanabe, Lieutenant Commander Y: 27-28, 44, 46, 50
Tanikaze: 58, 59
Togo, Admiral: 21
Tokyo: 6, 13, 20, 23, 47, 48
Tomano, Lieutenant: 23
Tomioka, Captain S: 6
Tomonaga, Lieutenant J: 27, 28, 29, 30, 39, 40-41, 42, 46, 48, 49
Tone: 22, 26, 28, 29, 30, 46
Tsushima, Battle of: 21
Tulagi: 13
Tyler, Captain M: 55

Ugaki, Rear Admiral M: 6, 17, 48, 50
US Combined Fleet: 6
  Fleet: 23, 28, 29, 47
  Intelligence: 17
  6th Battalion: 17
  Midway Command: 49
  Pacific Fleet: 6, 14, 15, 17, 18, 20, 23, 48, 50
  Task Force: 16, 20, 26, 30, 48
  Task: 17, 20, 26, 27, 30, 37, 48

Val: 27, 37
Vindicator: 55-56
Vireo: 44

Wada, Commander Y: 46

Wake Island: 23, 56, 59
Waldron, Lieutenant Commander J: 32
Watanabe, Commander Y: 6
Wildcat fighter plane: 30, 31, 39, 40, 41

Yamaguchi, Rear Admiral T: 22, 37, 39, 40, 41, 42, 46
Yamamoto, Admiral I: 6, 7, 15, 17, 18, 20, 21, 22, 23, 24, 30, 32, 35, 41, 42, 44, 46, 47, 48, 50, 51, 55, 59
Yamashiro: 20, 23
Yamato: 6, 15, 17, 20, 21, 23, 46, 47, 48, 50, 59
Yanagimoto, Captain R: 36
Yokosuka: 21
Yorktown: 13, 17, 18, 20, 21, 23, 26, 27, 29, 30, 31-42, 34, 37-39, 40-41, 42-44, 47, 48, 50
  Class: 40, 44

Zero fighter: 18, 27, 28, 29, 30, 32, 37, 39, 41, 49
Zuiho: 15, 23, 47, 59
Zuikaku: 13, 17

Acknowledgments
The author would like to thank the following individuals who helped prepare this book:

Jane Laslett, the editor
Adrian Hodgkins, the designer
Anthony Robinson for writing the captions
Penny Murphy for preparing the index

Picture Credits
The author would like to thank the individuals and agencies listed below for the use of their photographs and artworks.

John Batchelor: pp 52-3 (top and bottom)
Bison Picture Library: 15 (center), 16 (top), 49 (top), 56
Helen Downton: pp 56-7 (center)
Robert Hunt Library: pp 7 (center left and center right), 10 (bottom), 15 (top), 18 (bottom), 21, 22-3 (top), 26, 37, 39 (top), 41 (top), 46-7, 51
Imperial War Museum: pp 9, 12-3 (bottom), 14 (bottom), 15 (bottom), 16 (bottom), 22-3 (bottom), 28, 40 (bottom), 43 (top), 45 (top)
Kantosha Company: p 33 (bottom left)
via Koku-fan: pp 33 (center), 34 (bottom), 49 (bottom)
McDonnell-Douglas Corporation: p 19 (top left)
Richard Natkiel: pp 14 (top), 35
Wiley Noble: p 19 (top right)
Pilot Press: pp 55, 57 (top and center)
Mike Trim: pp 56-7 (bottom)
US Air Force: 10 (top), 34 (top)
US National Archives: 7 (bottom), 11, 18 (top), 19 (bottom), 20 (top right), 20-1 (bottom), 24-5, 27, 28-9, 30-1, 33 (bottom right), 38, 39 (bottom), 40 (top), 41 (bottom), 43 (bottom), 45 (bottom), 48, 50, 54-5, 58-9
US Navy: pp 1, 2-3, 4-5, 6, 7 (center), 8, 8-9 (bottom), 12, 12-13 (top), 20 (top left), 33 (top), 36, 42, 44, 47 (top), 52-3